Much A[c] About Nothing

William Shakespeare

Notes and activities: Annie Fox
Series consultant: Peter Buckroyd

OXFORD

UNIVERSITY PRESS

Contents

Introduction

What are Oxford Literature Companions?

Oxford Literature Companions is a series designed to provide you with comprehensive support for popular set texts. You can use the Companion alongside your play, using relevant sections during your studies or using the book as a whole for revision.

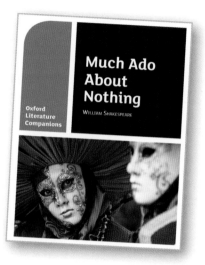

Each Companion includes detailed guidance and practical activities on:

- **Plot and Structure**
- **Context**
- **Characters**
- **Language**
- **Themes**
- **Performance**
- **Skills and Practice**

How does this book help with exam preparation?

As well as providing guidance on key areas of the play, throughout this book you will also find 'Upgrade' features. These are tips to help with your exam preparation and performance.

In addition, in the extensive **Skills and Practice** chapter, there is detailed guidance on areas such as how to prepare for the exam, understanding the question, planning your response and hints for what do to (or not do) in the exam.

In the **Skills and Practice** chapter there is also a bank of **Sample questions** and **Sample answers**. The **Sample answers** are marked and include annotations and a summative comment.

How does this book help with terminology?

Throughout the book, key terms are **highlighted** in the text and explained on the same page. There is also a detailed **Glossary** at the end of the book that explains, in the context of the play, all the relevant literary terms highlighted in this book.

Which edition of the play has this book used?

Quotations and character names have been taken from the Oxford University Press edition of *Much Ado About Nothing* (ISBN 978-0-19-832872-8).

How does this book work?

Each book in the Oxford Literature Companions series follows the same approach and includes the following features:

- **Key quotations** from the play
- **Key terms** explained on the page and linked to a complete glossary at the end of the book
- **Activity boxes** to help improve your understanding of the text
- **Upgrade** tips to help prepare you for your assessment

To help illustrate the features in this book, here are two annotated pages taken from this Oxford Literature Companion:

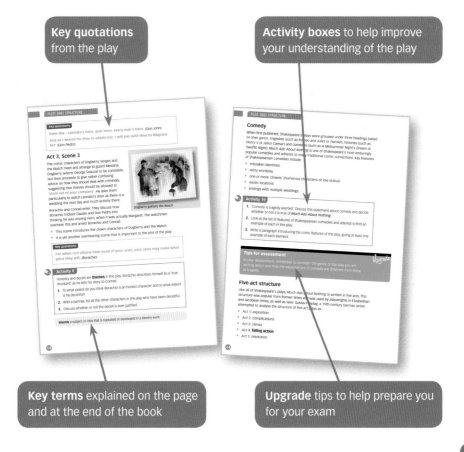

Key quotations from the play

Activity boxes to help improve your understanding of the play

Key terms explained on the page and at the end of the book

Upgrade tips to help prepare you for your exam

Plot and Structure

Plot

Set in Messina, Italy, Shakespeare's **comedy** *Much Ado About Nothing* revolves around the courtships and different experiences of love of two couples, Beatrice and Benedick, and Hero and Claudio. The title has been interpreted in many ways. It could indicate that this is a light-hearted play about nothing in particular or it could be **wordplay** on the word 'nothing', which was pronounced the same way as 'noting' in Elizabethan times and meant overhearing or perceiving. Much of the **plot** involves characters misunderstanding what they have overheard and so causing 'much ado' or a fuss about nothing.

Act 1, Scene 1

Leonato, the governor of Messina, his daughter Hero and his niece Beatrice receive happy news from a messenger that Don Pedro of Aragon and his soldiers are returning after a successful battle and will stay in Messina. In a teasing fashion, Beatrice asks the messenger how Benedick has done in the war. When Don Pedro, Benedick, Claudio, Balthasar and Don John arrive, it is clear that there is an old rivalry between Benedick and Beatrice, who he calls 'Lady Disdain'. Claudio declares himself to be in love with Hero: 'In mine eye she is the sweetest lady that ever I looked on' and he hopes to marry her. However Benedick states 'I will live a bachelor.' Don Pedro promises to woo Hero in disguise on behalf of Claudio at the party that evening.

- The opening, with its witty **dialogue** and lively atmosphere, establishes the play as a comedy, focused on love.

- The two contrasting romantic couples of Benedick and Beatrice, and Claudio and Hero, are introduced. The dialogue between Benedick and Beatrice suggests a tempestuous past relationship which has affected them both, whereas Claudio and Hero don't seem to know each other well, though Claudio claims that he 'lik'd her ere I went to wars'.

- Don John, the **antagonist** of the play, is briefly introduced and provides a contrast to the otherwise merry mood of the first scene.

> **antagonist** a character who is hostile to another character and tries to bring about his or her downfall
>
> **comedy** a genre of play which emphasizes the comic and amusing aspects of the characters' lives and ends happily
>
> **dialogue** the conversations of the characters
>
> **plot** the main events of the play
>
> **wordplay** witty use of words to play upon their multiple or unclear meanings

Activity 1

Look closely at Benedick's lines from **'That I neither feel how she should be loved...'** to **'Here you may see Benedick, the married man.'** Sum up Benedick's attitude towards women, love and marriage.

Key quotations

What, my dear Lady Disdain! Are you yet living? *(Benedick)*

You always end with a jade's trick. I know you of old. *(Beatrice)*

But I hope you have no intent to turn husband, have you? *(Benedick)*

... let them signify under my sign 'Here you may see Benedick, the married man.' *(Benedick)*

Act 1, Scene 2

Antonio, Leonato's brother, tells Leonato that Don Pedro, the Prince was overheard saying that he loved Hero and, if he found Hero 'accordant', was planning to tell Leonato of it. Leonato is excited at the prospect of this advantageous marriage and begins making arrangements for that evening's party.

- This is the first misunderstanding in the play because Antonio thinks Don Pedro is wooing Hero for himself rather than for Claudio.
- This **foreshadows** Claudio's later jealousy when he too thinks the Prince wants Hero for himself rather than acting as an ambassador for Claudio.
- It also foreshadows the later comic 'overhearing' scenes.

Activity 2

Leonato refers to this as a **'busy time'**. Imagine you are directing this scene. What do you think the actor playing Leonato might be busy doing?

Key quotations

We will hold it as a dream till it appear itself.

foreshadow when an author hints at something which happens later

Act 1, Scene 3

Don John, Don Pedro's illegitimate brother, is urged by his companion Conrad to appear happier since he is back in his brother's favour after a period when he had 'stood out' against him. Don John declares himself to be a 'plain-dealing villain', who wants to make mischief. Borachio says that he has overheard Don Pedro's plan to woo Hero for Claudio and Don John hopes to 'cross him any way'.

- After his almost mute first appearance, Don John reveals his evil character.
- The Prince and Claudio's conversation was overheard by yet another character, but this time was correctly interpreted.
- This gives Don John a chance to sow the seeds of jealousy in Claudio.

Activity 3

The mood of this scene is very different from the two preceding scenes. How would you stage and costume this scene to emphasize the darker mood of Don John? Create a storyboard, drawing a simple sketch for each line below. In each sketch, show where you would position Don John on stage in relation to the other characters and represent his posture, gestures and facial expressions.

a) 'I cannot hide what I am.'

b) 'If I had my mouth I would bite.'

c) 'Will it serve for any model to build mischief on?'

d) 'You are both sure, and will assist me?'

Key quotations

I had rather be a canker in a hedge than a rose in his grace. *(Don John)*

Therefore I have decreed not to sing in my cage. *(Don John)*

That young start-up hath all the glory of my overthrow. *(Don John)*

Tips for assessment

In only three scenes, Act 1 has established a number of key plot points. When writing about the plot, remember not just to retell the story but to look at when characters are introduced and in what order events are revealed. For example, in the first Act we have three versions of Don Pedro's wooing of Hero: his suggestion to do this; Antonio's misunderstanding of his intentions and Don John's correct understanding which he will then twist into something false.

Act 2, Scene 1

After supper, Leonato and his guests gather for a masked dance. Beatrice makes scornful remarks about Benedick and Don John, and is warned that she may never get a husband as she is 'so shrewd' of tongue. With the characters in disguises, they divide into couples. During these encounters, Don Pedro speaks privately to Hero, Balthasar flirts with Margaret, Ursula teases Antonio, and Beatrice and Benedick spar verbally. Meanwhile, Don John tells Claudio that Don Pedro has wooed Hero for himself, which makes Claudio jealous. The annoyed Benedick complains to Don Pedro that Beatrice has 'misused' him. Calming the jealous Claudio, Don Pedro makes clear that he has arranged the marriage between Claudio and Hero, obtaining Leonato's 'good will'. The young couple agree to marry, with Leonato's happy consent. Don Pedro and Beatrice have a playful conversation in which he appears to offer to be her husband: 'Will you have me, lady?' She turns him down with a joke. Don Pedro concocts a scheme in order to make the self-proclaimed bachelor Benedick fall in love with Beatrice.

- Claudio's emotional and jealous nature is exposed in this scene.
- The verbal sparring between Benedick and Beatrice heightens.
- The plan to trick Benedick and Beatrice into falling in love is formed.

The masked ball gives some characters the opportunity to speak honestly and freely, whilst others try to make mischief; National Theatre production 1981

Key quotations

He that hath a beard is more than a youth, and he that hath no beard is less than a man; and he that is more than a youth is not for me, and he that is less than man, I am not for him. *(Beatrice)*

O God, sir, here's a dish I love not. I cannot endure my Lady Tongue. *(Benedick)*

Silence is the perfectest herald of joy. *(Claudio)*

My lord, if they were but a week married they would talk themselves mad. *(Leonato)*

Activity 4

Create a chart like the one below, listing all the insults that Benedick and Beatrice hurl at each other and what they mean.

Beatrice about Benedick	What it means	Benedick about Beatrice	What it means
'evermore tattling'	He talks too much.	'disdainful'	She's proud, thinks too much of herself and not enough of others.
'prince's jester'		'base and bitter disposition'	

Act 2, Scene 2

Seeing that their mischief in spoiling the match between Claudio and Hero was short-lived, Borachio and Don John hatch a more elaborate scheme in which Borachio will call Margaret 'Hero' and appear to be making love to 'Hero' in order to dishonour the real Hero. Don John agrees to pay Borachio a thousand ducats for successfully arranging this plot, which will ruin Claudio and Hero's engagement and tarnish the honour of all involved.

- Borachio and Don John's second plot is revealed. This plot could be seen as a darker, more dangerous version of the playful overhearing scene which follows it.
- Don John's character is further revealed as being willing to do anything to 'despite' his brother and his brother's friends.

Key quotations

What life is in that to be the death of this marriage? *(Don John)*

Proof enough to misuse the prince, to vex Claudio, to undo Hero and kill Leonato. *(Borachio)*

Activity 5

Don John and Borachio use negative words associated with illness, poison and death in this scene.

1. Locate and list these words.

2. Then write a paragraph explaining how this use of language makes it clear that these two characters are the villains of the play.

Act 2, Scene 3

Alone in an orchard, Benedick has a **soliloquy**, musing on how Claudio has changed from a soldier who laughed at those who were in love to someone who is now in love himself. Benedick asserts that he will never be made 'such a fool'.

When Don Pedro, Leonato and Claudio enter the garden to hear Balthasar sing, Benedick hides to overhear what they say. Knowing that Benedick is eavesdropping, the men pretend that they have been told that Beatrice is tormented by love for

Benedick. Don Pedro lists Beatrice's many virtues and how she is wise 'in everything but in loving Benedick'. They claim they will not tell Benedick of Beatrice's love yet. They leave, secretly confident that their plan to fool Benedick will succeed.

Benedick delivers a second soliloquy in which he decides that this is 'no trick' and that Beatrice's love must be **'requited'**. When Beatrice enters ungraciously against her will to call him to dinner, Benedick believes that he can 'spy some marks of love in her'.

Humour heightens the dramatic irony as Benedick hides to overhear what his friends say, as shown in the National Theatre production of 1981

- This famous 'overhearing' or **'gulling'** scene is rich in **dramatic irony** as the audience is aware that Benedick is being set up by his friends to fall in love with Beatrice.

- Music is used to heighten the mood and explore the relationship between the sexes.

- Much humour is derived by Benedick's sudden change in attitude from his first soliloquy in which he declares his aversion to marriage to his declaration in the second that he will be 'horribly in love with her'.

dramatic irony when the audience knows something one or more characters on stage do not, e.g. the audience knows that Benedick's friends know he is there and that they are purposely trying to convince him that Beatrice is in love with him

gulling tricking or deceiving

requited something returned in equal measure, such as love

soliloquy when a character is alone, speaking his or her thoughts to the audience

Key quotations

But till all graces be in one woman, one woman shall not come in my grace. *(Benedick)*

No. The world must be peopled. When I said I would die a bachelor, I did not think I should live till I were married. *(Benedick)*

Activity 6

This scene is a favourite for creating '**comic business**'.

1. With a partner, discuss what might be on stage in this scene (e.g. trees, a fountain, benches).

2. Decide all the places where Benedick could hide and when he might almost be 'caught' by his friends.

3. What staging ideas would contribute to the humour and clarity of the scene?

Tips for assessment

All **stage directions** in Shakespeare's plays have been added by editors and vary from edition to edition, but Shakespeare often suggests the movements of the characters in the dialogue. Read Act 2, Scene 3 and Act 3, Scene 1 carefully, noting the stage directions in your edition of the play and what movements are implied by the dialogue.

Act 3, Scene 1

Hero sends Margaret to fetch Beatrice so that Beatrice can overhear Hero and Ursula gossiping about her. Once Beatrice hides, Hero and Ursula discuss how Beatrice is too '**disdainful**' to know that Benedick loves her '**so entirely**'. They praise Benedick as going '**foremost in report through Italy**' but say that Beatrice would only '**mock**' them if they told her. Beatrice ends the scene with a short soliloquy, declaring that she will love Benedick.

● This scene mirrors the previous scene, but with the genders reversed.

● The comedy of Beatrice ineffectively hiding in the orchard is a highlight of the scene.

● Like Benedick, Beatrice undergoes a radical change in attitude towards love.

comic business physical movements and gestures, sometimes involving props or set pieces, which heighten the humour of a scene

stage direction part of the script, but not the speeches, which gives indications of the setting and physical actions. Editors of Shakespeare's plays use stage directions to establish entrances, exits and other key movements such as fights

Key quotations

Of this matter
Is little Cupid's crafty arrow made,
That only wounds by hearsay. *(Hero)*

And, Benedick, love on. I will requite thee,
Taming my wild heart to thy loving hand. *(Beatrice)*

Activity 7

Look closely at Hero's speech which begins **'Why, you speak truth...'**.

1. In your own words, rewrite this speech to demonstrate what Beatrice's attitude to men has been in the past.

2. Why do you think she holds these beliefs and what does this tell you about her as a character?

Tips for assessment

When writing about a comedy, consider how comic effects are achieved. For example, does the comedy build and develop by having the two overhearing scenes follow so closely together?

Act 3, Scene 2

Don Pedro, Leonato and Claudio tease Benedick about his changed attitude and appearance. Benedick asks Leonato to **'walk aside with me'**, presumably to discuss Beatrice. Don John enters and announces that Hero is **'disloyal'**. He invites Claudio to go to Hero's chamber window that night to confirm her **'wickedness'**.

- The mood in this scene rapidly changes from playful to serious.

- The scene ends on an ominous note with the characters commenting on the sudden transformation of events.

- This scene is considered a turning point, when the play turns from purely comic to potentially tragic.

Activity 8

Don John is uncomfortable in Messina society. When he is on stage, there is often a coldness and awkwardness with other characters, which could be caused partly by his illegitimate status and partly by his personal characteristics.

1. Look at his lines and the brief replies to him given by Don Pedro in this scene.

2. Then write a paragraph describing how the actors should emphasize their distant relationship.

> **Key quotations**
>
> Even she – Leonato's Hero, your Hero, every man's Hero. *(Don John)*
>
> And as I wooed for thee to obtain her, I will join with thee to disgrace her. *(Don Pedro)*

Act 3, Scene 3

The comic characters of Dogberry, Verges and the Watch meet and arrange to guard Messina. Dogberry selects George Seacoal to be constable, but then proceeds to give rather confusing advice on how they should deal with criminals, suggesting that thieves should be allowed to 'steal out of your company'. He asks them particularly to watch Leonato's door as there is a wedding the next day and much activity there.

Dogberry gathers the Watch

Borachio and Conrad enter. They discuss how Borachio tricked Claudio and Don Pedro into thinking he was wooing Hero, when it was actually Margaret. The watchmen overhear this and arrest Borachio and Conrad.

- This scene introduces the clown characters of Dogberry and the Watch.
- It is yet another overhearing scene that is important to the plot of the play.

> **Key quotations**
>
> For when rich villains have need of poor ones, poor ones may make what price they will. *(Borachio)*

Activity 9

Honesty and deceit are **themes** in the play. Borachio describes himself as a 'true drunkard' as he tells his story to Conrad.

1. To what extent do you think Borachio is an honest character and to what extent is he deceitful?
2. With a partner, list all the other characters in the play who have been deceitful.
3. Discuss whether or not the deceit is ever justified.

theme a subject or idea that is repeated or developed in a literary work

Act 3, Scene 4

On the morning of Hero's wedding, she is being dressed by her gentlewomen, Ursula and Margaret, who are teasing her about her wedding night. Beatrice enters with a bad cold and is also teased by Margaret. The women leave for the church.

- This short scene demonstrates the playful way the female characters interact with each other, including some **ribald** jokes, particularly from Margaret.
- There is dramatic irony in that these characters are unaware that Hero has been dishonoured in the male characters' eyes.

> **Key quotations**
>
> God give me joy to wear it, for my heart is exceeding heavy. *(Hero)*
>
> A maid, and stuffed! There's goodly catching of cold! *(Margaret)*

> **Activity 10**
>
> In this scene we see how the female characters are behaving on the morning of the wedding. In a small group, create a short role-play showing what preparations characters like Don John, Claudio and Don Pedro might be making at the same time.

Act 3, Scene 5

Dogberry and Verges intrude upon Leonato's preparations for the wedding to report the arrest they made, but do so in such a confusing and 'tedious' fashion that Leonato rushes off to the church before hearing their news.

- This scene provides more examples of the comic misuse of words by Dogberry and Verges, which sometimes leads to misunderstandings.
- The comedy of this scene contrasts with the potential tragedy of the following denunciation of Hero in the church.
- This is another example of dramatic irony because the audience is aware of the importance of what Dogberry wants to tell Leonato, but he is not.

> **Key quotations**
>
> Our watch, sir, have indeed comprehended two auspicious persons, and we would have them this morning examined before your worship. *(Dogberry)*

ribald crude humour, usually involving jokes about sex

> **Activity 11**
>
> 'If only Leonato had listened!' Write a paragraph explaining how the play would
> have been very different if only Leonato had listened to Dogberry and Verges.

Act 4, Scene 1

The wedding party has gathered in the church where Hero and Claudio are to be
married by Friar Francis. During the ceremony, Claudio denounces Hero and refuses
to marry her, saying that she is a 'rotten orange' and that she has known 'the
heat of a luxurious bed'. Hero wonders who can 'blot' her name with any 'just
reproach' and denies that she had spoken to a man at her window. However, her
father believes Don Pedro's and Claudio's accusations. Hero collapses and her
accusers exit.

Beatrice defends Hero against the accusations and Benedick counsels patience. To
protect Hero's reputation, the Friar suggests that they say that Hero 'died upon
[Claudio's] words', giving them time to either prove her innocence or, failing that, to
'conceal her... in some reclusive and religious life'.

Left alone in the church, Benedick and Beatrice declare their love for each other.
Benedick offers to do anything for Beatrice and she responds, 'Kill Claudio.' Beatrice
insists that Hero has been wronged and Benedick agrees to challenge him.

- This scene contrasts the two romantic couples with Claudio and Hero falling
  apart dramatically and Benedick and Beatrice, to their mutual surprise and
  pleasure, coming together.
- The themes of love and violence are apparent in both couples' interactions.
- This scene reads much like a tragedy and bears some resemblance to scenes in
  Romeo and Juliet.

Claudio denounces
Hero, in the
Shakespeare's Globe
production in 2011

> **Key quotations**
>
> There, Leonato, take her back again.
> Give not this rotten orange to your friend! *(Claudio)*
>
> O Fate, take not away thy heavy hand.
> Death is the fairest cover for her shame *(Leonato)*
>
> I do love nothing in the world so well as you. Is not that strange?
> *(Benedick)*
>
> I cannot be a man with wishing; therefore I will die a woman with
> grieving. *(Beatrice)*

Activity 12

Use a chart like the one below to contrast Hero and Claudio's relationship with that of Benedick and Beatrice.

	Hero and Claudio	Evidence from text	Beatrice and Benedick	Evidence from text
How they fall in love	Quickly, almost upon first sight		After being tricked by their friends	
How they speak to each other				
What they say about each other				
How they speak about love				
How the relationship changes in this scene				

Tips for assessment

This scene is a pivotal one in the play, when there is a dramatic change in the relationships between the characters. When writing about it, note its tragic potential and importance in the play.

Act 4, Scene 2

Dogberry, Verges and the Sexton gather to interrogate the prisoners, Borachio and Conrad, and to hear the evidence of the Watch, who reveal that Borachio received a thousand ducats from Don John **'for accusing the Lady Hero wrongfully'**. The Sexton confirms that the prisoners must be bound and brought to Leonato. Conrad calls Dogberry **'an ass'**.

- This is another comic scene in which Dogberry's good intentions but clumsy delivery are revealed.
- The plot is now hastening towards its satisfactory resolution.

Activity 13

1. Write a paragraph in which you highlight the different characteristics of the main characters in this scene: Dogberry, the Sexton, Conrad and Borachio.

2. How does Shakespeare differentiate these characters through their actions and the way they speak?

Act 5, Scene 1

In conference with Antonio, Leonato expresses his grief about Hero's situation, while his brother counsels patience. Don Pedro and Claudio enter, and Leonato quarrels with them. After the older men exit, Benedick enters and is greeted cheerfully by Don Pedro and Claudio.

Benedick challenges Claudio saying, **'You have killed a sweet lady, and her death shall fall heavy on you.'** He also tells Don Pedro that he must **'discontinue'** his company and that Don Pedro and Claudio bear the responsibility for Hero's death, especially as it is now known that Don John has fled Messina.

Dogberry enters with his prisoners and Borachio confesses to Don Pedro his role in duping them into thinking Hero was unfaithful. Leonato enters and blames Don Pedro, Claudio and the absent Don John for his daughter's death. Claudio invites him to choose his revenge. Leonato replies that Claudio must marry Hero's 'cousin', who is **'Almost the copy of my child that's dead'.** Claudio agrees.

- This scene moves rapidly and fluently from one set of characters to the next, setting up the play's ultimate resolution.
- A different side of Benedick is exposed in his denunciation of his former friends' actions.
- This is Dogberry's last scene in the play in which he adds both to the play's resolution and its comedy.

> **Key quotations**
>
> My villainy they have upon record, which I had rather seal with my death than repeat over to my shame. *(Borachio)*
>
> Hang her an epitaph upon her tomb
> And sing it to her bones; sing it tonight. *(Leonato)*

Activity 14

There are many shifting moods in this scene. Using a table like the one below, break down the scene into sections. Identify the mood of each section and the evidence from the text that suggests it.

Section	Mood	Evidence from text
Antonio and Leonato – the brothers speak privately		
Leonato, Antonio, Don Pedro and Claudio – conflict between the men		
Benedick, Claudio and Don Pedro – conflict between Benedick and his friends		
Dogberry, Verges, the Watch, Conrad and Borachio – Dogberry as an unlikely hero		
Borachio's confession		
Leonato's 'revenge'		
Dogberry's exit		

Tips for assessment

Upgrade

When thinking about mood, reflect on the emotional tone of the scene. Some moods you may discover in this play are: angry, bitter, humorous, tense, romantic, boisterous, uneasy, secretive, celebratory, penitent or confrontational.

Beatrice and Benedick tease each other, in the National Theatre production in 2007

Act 5, Scene 2

Benedick asks for Margaret's help in writing a poem to Beatrice. She exits in order to bring Beatrice to him and, alone on stage, he sings a love song. He breaks off and bemoans his inability to find appropriate rhymes. Beatrice enters and they speak teasingly to each other, causing Benedick to exclaim, **'Thou and I are too wise to woo peaceably.'** Ursula enters to tell them that Hero's reputation has been restored.

● This scene demonstrates how the 'too wise' Benedick and Beatrice will never be a conventional romantic pair.

● The scene explores how romantic words do not necessarily reveal true love.

> **Key quotations**
>
> I will live in thy heart, die in thy lap, and be buried in thy eyes; and, moreover, I will go with thee to thy uncle's. *(Benedick)*

Activity 15

Looking closely at the dialogue from Beatrice's entrance to her line ending '... **for I will never love that which my friend hates**', note how many times Beatrice threatens to leave during this scene. Rehearse the scene to explore how these threatened exits could be handled and what keeps Beatrice from leaving on each occasion.

Act 5, Scene 3

In Leonato's family's tomb, Claudio performs the rites of honour to the 'dead' Hero. Balthasar sings a song, and Claudio and Don Pedro depart in order to prepare for the next wedding.

- This scene shows Claudio displaying his penitence for having wronged Hero.
- Poetry and music are used to underscore the mood and meaning of the scene.

> **Key quotations**
>
> And **Hymen** now with luckier issue speeds
> Than this for whom we render'd up this woe. *(Claudio)*

Activity 16

Create a spider diagram like the one below. On each leg, write a quotation from the play that gives an image of what it is like in the tomb. Some have been given to you, but you can add others. Then explain what effect each has on the audience.

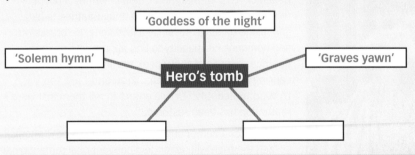

Hymen the Greek god of marriage

Act 5, Scene 4

In the play's final scene, the characters gather again for a wedding. Claudio has agreed to marry Hero's 'cousin' and all the female characters enter the church masked, making it unclear which is his bride. Antonio presents the masked Hero to Claudio, who says, 'I am your husband, if you like of me.' Unmasking herself, Hero reveals that she is alive.

Benedick asks which of the women is Beatrice and when she unmasks herself, he asks her if she loves him. She at first tries to deny this, as he does his love, but their friends show love **sonnets** that each has written to the other. Benedick declares this 'A miracle! Here's our own hands against our hearts.' The parties prepare for a double wedding.

A messenger enters with news that Don John is being returned by armed men to Messina. Benedick urges them not to think about him until the next day and the play ends with a dance.

- Benedick completes his transformation by urging Don Pedro to 'get thee a wife'.
- The play's resolution neatly ties together most of the loose ends of the plot, uniting the lovers and promising punishment for the villain.

> **sonnet** a 14-line poem with a formal rhyme scheme. In Shakespearean sonnets, the first 12 lines rhyme alternately and then end with a rhyming couplet

Claudio agrees to marry Hero's 'cousin', in the Peter Hall production at Bath Theatre Royal, in 2005

Key quotations

How dost thou, 'Benedick the married man'? *(Don Pedro)*

For man is a giddy thing, and this is my conclusion. *(Benedick)*

Activity 17

The Victorian playwright Oscar Wilde famously wrote, 'The good ended happily and the bad unhappily. That is what Fiction means.'

Do you believe that the good characters in the play have ended happily and that the evil characters have been appropriately punished? Write a two-minute speech explaining how much you think the ending of *Much Ado About Nothing* is just and fair.

Structure

Handling of time

The action of the play is compressed and the initial rush for Hero and Claudio to be married on so short an acquaintance is key to the plot. Claudio wants to be married 'tomorrow' though, at Leonato's insistence, he must wait a little longer than that. However, he is not the only impatient character: Leonato quickly assumes that it is the Prince rather than Claudio who wishes to marry Hero and similarly ignores Dogberry's discovery of the plot because he is too busy to listen. Upon the failure of his first plan to cause mischief, Don John hurriedly concocts a second plan with Borachio, which succeeds only briefly.

This is a summer play, as Don Pedro refers to 'the sixth of July' in his mocking formal closing to an imagined letter in the first scene. Although it is possible that only five or six individual days are depicted, it is evident that there are gaps between these days because in Act 2, Scene 1 Leonato insists that 'ten nights' watchings' will pass between the formal engagement of Hero and Claudio in that scene and the wedding in Act 4, Scene 1. In the gap between these events, Don Pedro decides to 'undertake one of Hercules' labours, which is to bring Senor Benedick and the Lady Beatrice into a mountain of affection th'one with th'other' *(Act 2, Scene 1)*. The two 'gulling' scenes occur one after the other in the play, but may actually be on different days within the play's timescale. It is also a matter for conjecture how much time passes between the breaking off of the marriage of Hero and Claudio and the Act 5 revelation of her innocence.

Activity 18

1. Create a table like the one below in order to establish the order and speed of key events.

Day	Key events	Key quotations
Day 1: daytime (probably 6 July, as indicated in Act 1, Scene 1)	• Leonato welcomes Don Pedro and his followers to his house. • Claudio falls in love with Hero. • Don John decides to cause mischief between Don Pedro and Claudio.	
Day 1: evening at the masked ball	• Don Pedro woos Hero for Claudio. • Benedick and Beatrice argue. • Don Pedro decides to trick Benedick into falling in love with Beatrice. • Don John and Borachio plan to spoil the wedding.	
Day 2	• The 'overhearing' scene in which Benedick is fooled	
Day 3	• The 'overhearing' scene in which Beatrice is fooled	
Day 3: evening	• Dogberry and the Watch meet, and the Watch discover Borachio's involvement in the scheme.	
Day 4: (ten days after day 1)	• Hero prepares for her wedding. • Dogberry tries to tell Leonato of the plot. • The wedding is broken off. • Beatrice and Benedick declare their love for each other.	
Day 5	• Benedick challenges Claudio. • The plot is revealed.	
Day 5: night	• Claudio hangs an epitaph in Hero's tomb.	
Day 6	• The double weddings and happy ending.	

2. On your table, highlight the 'comic' incidents and quotations in a light colour and the more dramatic, serious sections in a dark colour in order to explore how Shakespeare combines the different moods of the play.

Comedy

When first published, Shakespeare's plays were grouped under three headings based on their genre: tragedies (such as *Romeo and Juliet* or *Hamlet*), histories (such as *Henry V* or *Julius Caesar*) and comedies (such as *A Midsummer Night's Dream* or *Twelfth Night*). *Much Ado About Nothing* is one of Shakespeare's most enduringly popular comedies and adheres to many traditional comic conventions. Key features of Shakespearean comedies include:

- mistaken identities
- witty wordplay
- one or more 'clowns' (humorous characters of low status)
- exotic locations
- endings with multiple weddings.

Activity 19

1. 'Comedy is tragedy averted.' Discuss this statement about comedy and decide whether or not it is true of *Much Ado About Nothing*.

2. Look at the list of features of Shakespearean comedies and attempt to find an example of each in this play.

3. Write a paragraph introducing the comic features of the play, giving at least one example of each element.

Tips for assessment

In your assessment, remember to consider the genre of the play you are writing about and how the expectations of comedy are different from those of tragedy.

Five-act structure

Like all of Shakespeare's plays, *Much Ado About Nothing* is written in five acts. This structure was popular from Roman times and was used by playwrights in Elizabethan and Jacobean times, as well as later. Gustav Freytag, a 19th-century German writer, attempted to analyse the structure of five-act plays as:

- Act 1: exposition
- Act 2: complications
- Act 3: climax
- Act 4: **falling action**
- Act 5: resolution.

Although Freytag felt that each Act should represent one of these structural functions, Shakespeare's plays are more fluid than this and you may find that the plays do not always neatly fit into this pattern. For example, some complications might appear in the first Act, and the climax might be later than the third Act.

Activity 20

Using a table like the one below, analyse the structure of *Much Ado About Nothing*.

Structural function	Explanation
Exposition: Setting and characters are introduced and background information is supplied. Possible future actions and conflict are suggested.	• Act 1, Scene 1: Leonato's family are introduced in the first scene and the past feuding between Beatrice and Benedick is explored. • Claudio falls in love with Hero. • Act 1, Scene 3: Future conflict is suggested by Don John's **antipathy** for Don Pedro and Claudio.
Complications: Problems and conflicts occur. Events begin to speed up.	
Climax: The conflict reaches its tensest point. There may be a turning point that affects the outcome of the play.	• Act 4, Scene 1: Claudio denounces Hero.
Falling action: Consequences of the climax are felt.	
Resolution: The conflict is resolved and, in comedy, there is a happy ending.	

Plot and sub-plot

Given the importance of and interest in the characters of Benedick and Beatrice, it may surprise audiences that their story is nominally the **sub-plot** of the play, whereas the tortuous romance between Hero and Claudio is the main plot. The false accusation against Hero involves most of the characters, including Don John and Borachio, her accusers, and Friar Francis, Dogberry and Verges, her surprising saviours.

antipathy intense dislike

falling action the events after the plot's climax which eventually lead to the resolution

sub-plot a secondary, less important plot of the play

However, most audiences find themselves particularly involved in the romance between the warring lovers Benedick and Beatrice and these are the roles that attract leading actors. Benedick, in particular, dominates the stage, speaking the most lines (17% of the play), sharing his thoughts with the audience in soliloquies, while his relationship with Beatrice develops through a series of scenes, ultimately leading to a fresh sense of self-discovery. Claudio speaks 11% of the lines, fewer than Leonato or Don Pedro, and often remains a difficult character for audiences to engage with, due to his unsympathetic actions.

It might be helpful to think of the play as having two **parallel plots**, which both involve misunderstandings, deceit and overhearings. One dramatic plot centres on the deceit that drives Hero and Claudio apart, whereas the other comic plot uses deceit to bring Benedick and Beatrice together. However, as befitting a comedy, both end happily.

Activity 21

1. Create a graph like the one below. In one colour, plot the love relationship between Beatrice and Benedick. In another colour, plot the relationship between Hero and Claudio.

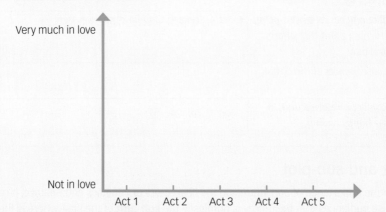

2. Using your graph, decide when the plots overlap. Then write a paragraph about the relationship between the two romances.

parallel plots plots that are woven together and usually share some characters and themes

Writing about structure

Upgrade

When writing about a play, it is important to demonstrate that you have understood its plot and structure. Even if you are only being asked to write about a particular scene or character, you need to refer to the play's form and structure, so you should consider the context of the scene or development of the character. However, do not simply retell the story of the play, but instead show how Shakespeare has created certain effects by the ordering and structuring of the scenes.

In order to improve your writing about structure and plot, consider doing the following:

- Write about how and when characters are introduced.
- Consider how comic effects, such as misunderstandings, sudden revelations or dramatic irony, are achieved by the structure of scenes.
- Discuss how the scenes are not purely comic but also contain the potential for tragedy.
- Highlight key scenes in which turning points or climaxes occur.
- Reflect on how the parallel plots of the lovers progress throughout the play.
- Consider how time is handled to increase suspense and excitement.
- Write about the play's 'happy ending' and any loose ends that are not entirely resolved.

Hero is promised in marriage to Claudio early on in the play, but as the plot unfolds, this is put in jeopardy

Biography of William Shakespeare

It is thought that Shakespeare (1564–1616) wrote *Much Ado About Nothing* in 1598

- Shakespeare was born in 1564, five years after the coronation of Queen Elizabeth I.

- He probably studied at the grammar school in Stratford-upon-Avon, learning subjects such as Latin **rhetoric** and literature until the age of about 15.

- In 1582 he married Anne Hathaway and they had three children: Susanna, Judith and Hamnet.

- By the early 1590s he had moved to London and begun to make a reputation for himself as an actor, poet and playwright.

- Although no one knows the exact chronology and dates of his plays, between 1595 and 1599 he is thought to have written many key texts including *Romeo and Juliet*, *The Merchant of Venice* and *Much Ado About Nothing*.

- Many of his greatest tragedies, including Hamlet, Othello and King Lear, were written in the period between 1599 and 1608.

- Shakespeare died in 1616 and is buried in Stratford-upon-Avon.

- In 1623 the **First Folio** edition of his plays was published.

Historical and cultural context

The historical period

Elizabeth I reigned over England from 1558–1603, a time of great discovery, artistic achievement and foreign adventure. Many critics feel that wherever and whenever Shakespeare set his plays, he was really writing about England in his own times. England was a powerful country, with confidence growing after the defeat of the Spanish Armada in 1588. It is perhaps no accident that this confidence is reflected in *Much Ado About Nothing*, which begins with a celebration of battle triumph and returning soldiers. Elizabethan audiences would also delight in seeing recognizable aspects of their society mirrored on stage, including the fashionable clothing of aristocratic characters, the interest in advantageous marriages and even the depiction of local government roles such as the constable of the Watch.

Elizabethan England was also a time of great contrasts. (Bill Bryson described London in the 16th century as 'deadly and desirable'.) Although there was high infant mortality and low life expectancy (around 35 years), the steady stream of arrivals to

> **First Folio** the name given to the edition of 36 of Shakespeare's plays published in 1623, which was prepared by two actors, John Heminges and Henry Condell
>
> **rhetoric** language designed to have a persuasive or impressive effect on its audience

London from rural locations and abroad kept the city growing. This caused concerns about public health and social unrest. Both of these issues sometimes led to the closing of the playhouses. In 1593, an outbreak of bubonic plague was reported to have killed more than 10,000 people in London, as well as resulting in the temporary closure of the London theatres such as the Globe.

The English Renaissance, from the late 15th century to the early 17th century, was a time when many art forms, including music, architecture and literature, flourished. Important writers during this golden age of literary arts include Christopher Marlowe (*Doctor Faustus*), Ben Jonson (*Volpone*), Edmund Spenser (*The Faerie Queen*) and Thomas Kyd (*The Spanish Tragedy*). Shakespeare's genius was noted by contemporaries with jealousy (fellow writer Robert Greene notoriously referred to Shakespeare as an 'upstart Crow') and admiration (Ben Jonson, a poet and playwright who knew Shakespeare well, wrote an epitaph for him in 1618 which declared, 'He was not of an age, but for all time!').

Tips for assessment

Upgrade

When writing about context, make sure your contextual information is correct – every year students lose marks by writing about the' Victorian' age, when they mean 'Elizabethan' or the '19th century' when they mean the '16th century'. Whatever you do, don't write about 'ye olden days'!

Sources

Shakespeare was an extremely prolific playwright who used a number of sources to inspire his plays. In *Much Ado About Nothing*, the plot concerning Hero and Claudio resembles many stories that were well known at the time in which a woman is wrongly accused of infidelity. One of the most likely sources of the play is the tale of Fenicia in Bandello's *La Prima Parte de la Nouvelle*, written in 1554. In this story, also set in Messina, the fiancé of an innocent young woman is deceived by a friend into believing that his love is receiving secret nightly visits from another lover. Like Hero, she also swoons, and her fiancé is told that she has died.

There are also traces of Aristo's poem, 'Orlando Furioso', written in 1516, in Shakespeare's play, particularly in the use of a maid (Dalinda in this tale). Like Margaret, she helps the villain to dishonour her lady (Genevra) by disguising herself as her mistress when meeting him in her mistress's bedchamber.

However, the Benedick and Beatrice part of the tale is not directly related to any known sources and seems to be an invention of Shakespeare's.

Patriarchy and marriage in Elizabethan times

Although Elizabeth I was not married, the country was still very much a **patriarchy** and the roles available to most women outside of marriage were limited. Women were not educated in schools, though they could, like Queen Elizabeth, be taught by private tutors. Most professions, such as law or medicine, were forbidden to them and they were not allowed to perform on stage. They could take on domestic jobs such as housekeepers, landladies and laundresses. In some cases, women could not inherit their father's estates, but others were allowed to be heir to their father's property, which made only daughters, like Hero, very desirable to suitors.

Marriages were usually arranged for couples by their families so that each family could benefit by gaining land or status. There was often a formal engagement, so when Claudio speaks the words 'Lady, as you are mine, I am yours' in Act 2, Scene 1, this could be considered a 'marriage by pre-contract'. The breaking of such an agreement would stain the reputation of those involved, particularly the bride and her relations. Women who did not marry were often treated with suspicion.

Activity 1

Using a table like the one below, read the quotations and then explain what they say about the characters' attitudes towards marriage.

Quotation	Attitude to marriage
Act 1, Scene 1 **Claudio:** Hath Leonato any son, my lord? **Don Pedro:** No child but Hero. She's his only heir.	Although Claudio has fallen in love with Hero, it is good news that she is also heir to her father's property. This would make her a desirable match and suitable for a count like Claudio.
Act 2, Scene 1 **Leonato:** By my troth, niece, thou wilt never get thee a husband if thou be so shrewd of thy tongue. **Antonio:** In faith, she's too curst.	
Act 2, Scene 1 **Leonato:** Daughter, remember what I told you. If the prince do solicit you in that kind, you know your answer.	
Act 2, Scene 1 **Leonato:** Count, take of me my daughter, and with her my fortunes. His grace hath made the match, and all grace say amen to it.	
Act 2, Scene 1 **Beatrice:** I may sit in a corner and cry 'Heigh-ho for a husband.'	
Act 5, Scene 4 **Benedick:** Prince, thou art sad. Get thee a wife, get thee a wife. There is no staff more reverend than one tipped with horn.	

patriarchy a society in which men are dominant

Similarities to other Shakespeare plays

In Shakespeare's time, Italy had a romantic and glamorous image. Shakespeare set many of his plays there, including *Romeo and Juliet*, *The Taming of the Shrew*, *A Winter's Tale*, *The Merchant of Venice* and, of course, *Much Ado About Nothing*. Some of these plays share not only an Italian location but other features such as a mixture of comedy and tragedy, strong female characters, the use of disguise and false deaths.

The 1993 film captured all the romance of the Italian setting

The critic M.C. Bradbrook wrote, 'If *Romeo and Juliet* was a tragedy with its full complement of comedy, and *The Merchant of Venice* a comedy with an infusion of tragic pity and fear, *Much Ado About Nothing* is a comedy… where deeper issues are overlaid with mirth… '. These three plays with Italian settings combine tragedy with comedy, with some critics saying that *Romeo and Juliet* bears more signs of comedy, with Mercutio's wit and the ribald Nurse, than tragedy until the deaths of Mercutio and Tybalt in Act 3. In Act 4, Scene 1 of *Much Ado About Nothing*, it seems the comedy may take a tragic turn, with Claudio's heart-felt damning of Hero and her desperate defence.

Disguise is also a common element in many of the plays. Both *Romeo and Juliet* and *Much Ado About Nothing* feature masked dances, whereas *The Merchant of Venice* has a number of characters, including Portia, Nerissa and Jessica, who assume disguises. These disguises can add to the festival atmosphere of the plays, but they can also represent opportunities for escape, deceit and misunderstandings.

Both Hero and Juliet are only daughters and the hopes of their families rest with them. However, the reactions of their fathers when they feel they have been deceived or thwarted are very strong, emphasizing the obedience that fathers expected from their daughters, including when it came to marriage. Both Beatrice in *Much Ado About Nothing* and Katherina in *The Taming of the Shrew* are single women in danger of becoming unmarriageable because of their strong personalities and reluctance to play a **subservient** role.

subservient submissive, willing to serve another or accept a secondary role

Social class

A clear hierarchy of social class existed in Elizabethan England, with Elizabeth I at the top and the poor at the bottom. The class structure was considered a vital component of social order and there were laws to ensure that rank and status were easily identifiable.

It was difficult to move from one social class to another, though people did gain status through advantageous marriages or acquiring land or wealth.

In the opening lines of the play the importance of social class is underlined by Leonato's question about how many 'gentlemen' were lost and the messenger's reply that few of 'rank' and 'none of name' died in the battle, implying that Leonato would only know and be concerned about the loss of soldiers of a certain class.

The monarch: The ruling king or queen.

Nobility: Powerful, rich landowners, often members of court and parliament.

Gentry: Aristocrats often of great wealth and owning some land.

Merchants: The tradespeople, artisans and shop owners.

Yeoman: Rural workers, such as farmers or shepherds.

Servants and labourers: Low-paid hired workers

The poor and homeless: Beggars or others who were unable to work.

Social order in Elizabethan England

Activity 2

In *Much Ado About Nothing*, social status is very important. Consider how pleased Leonato is when he thinks the Prince, Don Pedro, wishes to marry Hero. He is also happy for her to marry a count, such as Claudio, especially as the Prince has vouched for him. His reaction would undoubtedly be very different if he thought Hero's suitor was Dogberry.

1. Look at the list of characters for *Much Ado About Nothing* and number them in order of status. For example, Don Pedro is a prince, suggesting he has the highest status of all the characters, so put '1' next to his name. Indicate the status of all the other characters and be ready to explain your reasoning.

2. Locate any lines in the play in which a character is treated in a particular way due to his or her place in society.

Writing about context

Upgrade

When writing about context, it is important to show how your understanding of the time in which the play was written increases your appreciation of elements of the play itself. You should not just bolt on dates and facts, but instead demonstrate your knowledge that Shakespeare made certain choices and his audience had specific expectations because of when the play was written and first performed.

Aspects of context you might consider are:

• whether there are any aspects of Shakespeare's life or other work that relate to the question you have been asked

• what the attitudes were towards marriage at the time and how this influences the characters' actions

• how Claudio, Benedick and Don Pedro's successes as soldiers might be viewed by an Elizabethan audience

• how the Italian setting might be perceived by a London audience in Shakespeare's time

• how Shakespeare altered his play from its original sources in order to address the interests of his audience

• how an audience today might perceive aspects of the play differently from an audience in Shakespeare's time.

Main characters

Benedick

Benedick is one of Shakespeare's most engaging and popular mature comic characters, lively and well-favoured enough to deserve his name, which derives from the Latin 'Benedictus' meaning he who is blessed. He is particularly appealing because, although he is a very admirable character held in high esteem by all but Beatrice (Ursula asserts that his 'valour / Goes foremost in report through Italy' and he deserves his good name as 'His excellence did earn it' *Act 3, Scene 1*), he is also a character who becomes aware of his own weaknesses and contradictions.

Interest in him is established before his entrance by Beatrice's cutting enquiries about him, complaining about his behaviour before he went to war and belittling his efforts at war. The messenger defends him by saying Benedick was 'A lord to a lord, a man to a man, stuffed with all honourable virtues' *(Act 1, Scene 1).* When he enters, the 'merry war' with Beatrice begins immediately. He calls her 'Lady Disdain' and pretends to be surprised that she is 'yet living' *(Act 1, Scene 1).* Shakespeare suggests that they have had a previous relationship when Beatrice asserts 'I know you of old' *(Act 1, Scene 1).*

However, *Much Ado About Nothing* is a play about second chances. Despite their past battles, they need only the encouragement of hearing that the other is in love with them to forget immediately their previous grievances. Benedick knows that his sudden about-face will be a source of merriment ('I may chance have some odd quirks and remnants of wit broken on me because I have railed so long against marriage'), but is determined to 'requite' Beatrice *(Act 2, Scene 3).*

Much of Benedick's comedy revolves around the dual aspect of his character as he is a man of good reputation and highly regarded but is also foolish and egotistical. He is a successful soldier, but he also ineffectively hides in an orchard to hear gossip. Although capable of the wittiest of wordplay, he becomes awkward and tongue-tied when in love. His first declaration to Beatrice, in Act 4, Scene 1, 'I do love nothing in the world so well as you. Is not that strange?' is usually greeted with laughter by the audience.

In Act 4, Benedick must choose between loyalty to his friends and his new love for Beatrice. He chooses Beatrice and challenges Claudio to a duel. This isolates him from his good friend Don Pedro, highlighting Benedick's transition from being a soldier, most comfortable amongst men, to being a lover devoted to a woman. In Act 5, Scene 2, Benedick is further brought down to earth by his inability to write a conventional love song. Shakespeare uses this scene to highlight the gap between those who profess themselves to be in love through verse and someone like Benedick, who is truly in love but 'cannot show it in rhyme' *(Act 5, Scene 2).* At the end of the play, it is Benedick who brings the comedy to a close with his playful declaration that 'man is a giddy thing'.

Activity 1

Benedick is both an admirable character and a comic one. Create a chart like the one below giving examples of when he is a character worthy of respect and when he behaves foolishly.

Admirable qualities	Example	Foolish qualities	Example
A good solider	'He hath done good service, lady, in these wars.' (Act 1, Scene 1)	Easily tricked	'This can be no trick' (Act 2, Scene 3)
Witty wordplay		Poor at rhymes	
Defends Hero		Boasts	
Recognizes Beatrice's good qualities		Has treated Beatrice badly in the past	

Activity 2

When they are left alone together in Act 4, Scene 1, Benedick declares his love for Beatrice.

1. Looking closely at the dialogue from **'Lady Beatrice, have you wept all this while?'** to **'You kill me to deny it. Farewell.'**, make notes about what you think Benedick is thinking during this scene.

2. Read through this dialogue, experimenting with pauses and changes of tone.

3. How do you think Benedick should react when Beatrice says **'Kill Claudio'**?

Beatrice

'[Beatrice is] a creature overflowing with joyousness, raillery itself being in her nothing more than an excess of animal spirits, tempered by passing through a soul of goodness'. *Liverpool Journal Review*, 2 May 1846

Beatrice is a character who has charmed generations of audiences with her wit, her sense of honour and her eventual self-discovery. She is Leonato's niece and Hero's cousin. Although Antonio is identified as Leonato's brother, he is not Beatrice's father and her role in the household is as Hero's friend and companion. She and Hero share a bedchamber (except notably on the night when Margaret entertains Borachio at Hero's bedchamber window) and they clearly have a friendly and informal relationship. Beatrice takes centre stage early in the play with her confident questioning of the messenger and continues with her sharp-tongued conversation with Benedick.

Beatrice and Benedick have previously had a relationship. At that time, she gave him 'a double heart for his single one', suggesting that she loved him twice as much as he did her, but he was 'false', which may explain the venom with which she verbally attacks him. However, after hearing a description of his love for her, the speed with which she decides to 'requite' Benedick implies that she has remained in love with him all along (*Act 3, Scene 1*).

Feminist critics often admire Beatrice's unwillingness to play a silent, modest, subservient role in a society in which that was considered the ideal. Instead she is bold, loyal, quick-witted and fallible, ultimately making a match that would seem to be between two equals.

The characters of Benedick and Beatrice have captured hearts throughout the ages

---

Key quotations

I had rather hear my dog bark at a crow than a man swear he loves me. (*Beatrice, Act 1, Scene 1*)

Indeed, my lord, he lent it me a while, and I gave him use of it, a double heart for his single one. Marry, once before he won it of me with false dice. Therefore your grace may well say I have lost it. (*Beatrice, Act 2, Scene 1*)

I love you with so much of my heart that none is left to protest. (*Beatrice, Act 4, Scene 1*)

---

feminist critic an academic writer who analyses works, looking particularly at the portrayal of female characters and issues of inequality in gender roles

Activity 3

In plays, characterization is achieved by what characters say, what they do and what others say about them.

Look closely at the lines below when other characters describe Beatrice. Create a similar table, analysing what these lines tells us about her as a character.

Who says it	What is said	What this tells us about Beatrice
Leonato	'merry war betwixt Signor Benedick and her… a skirmish of wit between them' (Act 1, Scene 1)	*She is willing to battle with Benedick and they match wits.*
Benedick	'It is the base and bitter disposition of Beatrice that puts the world into her person, and so give me out.' '… while she is here a man may live as quiet in hell as in a sanctuary, and people sin upon purpose because they would go thither. So indeed all disquiet, horror, and perturbation follows her.' (Act 2, Scene 1)	
Don Pedro	'… you were born in a merry hour.' 'By my troth, a pleasant-spirited lady.' (Act 2, Scene 1)	
Benedick	'They say the lady is fair; 'tis a truth, can bear them witness. And virtuous; 'tis so, I cannot reprove it. And wise, but for loving me.' (Act 2, Scene 3)	
Hero	'Disdain and scorn ride sparkling in her eyes / Misprising what they look on, and her wit / Values itself so highly that to her / All matter else seems weak. She cannot love, / Nor take no shape nor project affection, / She is so self-endear'd.' (Act 3, Scene 1)	

Activity 4

Due to her outspokenness and unwillingness to conform to the expectations of women in her society, Beatrice is sometimes considered a **feminist icon**. Write a speech in which you argue either for or against the following proposition: 'The character of Beatrice is a feminist icon – until she falls in love.'

feminist icon someone who is a positive role model for women, e.g. by show of strength, intelligence or independence beyond what is expected in her society

Don Pedro

Don Pedro is the victorious Prince of Aragon, whose decision to stop in Messina is a catalyst for the play's plot. His important social function is reinforced by the many times he is referred to as the 'prince' and by the delight that Leonato expresses when he mistakenly believes that Don Pedro wishes to marry his daughter Hero. He has 'bestowed much honour' upon Claudio for his successes as a soldier and recommends Claudio as Hero's bridegroom *(Act 1, Scene 1)*, causing Leonato to say 'his grace hath made the match, and all grace say amen to it' *(Act 2, Scene 1)*. Don Pedro's reputation is very important to him and he feels 'dishonoured' when he believes he has made an inappropriate match for his friend.

Don Pedro can be seen as a contradictory character. He is clearly at odds with his illegitimate brother Don John, whom he has recently defeated, and yet he introduces him to Messina society and immediately believes his slanders about Hero. He also plays a vital role in bringing both couples together. Yet at the end of the play he remains alone. His 'proposal' to Beatrice in Act 2, Scene 1 ('Will you have me, lady?') can be interpreted as a sincere proposal, an act of gallantry or simply a question about Beatrice's desires.

Activity 5

Read the dialogue in Act 2, Scene 1 from 'Good Lord, for alliance!' to 'Cousins, God give you joy.' experimenting with the **sub-text** of the scene. Try the following ways of interpreting the scene:

- as if Don Pedro is really in love with Beatrice and is very hurt when she says 'No, my lord'

- as if Don Pedro is teasing Beatrice in response to her saying she would like his brother

- as if Don Pedro is surprised by what Beatrice says and suddenly wonders if he should marry her.

Decide which interpretation works best in your opinion and why.

Activity 6

At the end of the play, Benedick urges Don Pedro to 'get thee a wife' *(Act 5, Scene 4)*. Imagine that Shakespeare had written a short speech for Don Pedro to reply to this, then write what you think it might say.

sub-text the meaning beneath words, not directly stated

Leonato

Leonato is Governor of Messina, Hero's father and Beatrice's uncle. His lively household, with its servants, gardens, parties and musicians, is central to the play. In the first acts of the play, we frequently see him in a celebratory mood: greeting visitors, preparing for a party or arranging a wedding. However, in Act 4, Scene 1, he changes from a doting father to an outraged one. He even wishes that Hero would die: 'Do not live, Hero, do not ope thine eyes'. However, by Act 5, although still awaiting proof of her innocence, he believes that Hero 'is belied' and feistily confronts Claudio and Don Pedro *(Act 5, Scene 1)*. By the end of the play, he has the happy wedding he was planning for and his final line is a return to his previously joyous self, 'We'll have dancing afterward.' *(Act 5, Scene 4)*.

> **Key quotations**
>
> Bring me a father that so lov'd his child,
> Whose joy of her is overwhelm'd like mine,
> And bid him speak of patience. *(Leonato, Act 5, Scene 1)*

Activity 7

Leonato can be seen as an impetuous, impatient character, who sometimes acts or speaks before he thinks. Find as many instances as you can when Leonato's impulsiveness or rashness is presented in the play.

Claudio

Claudio is a young Florentine nobleman who has distinguished himself during the recent wars, impressing Don Pedro. Upon arrival in Messina he falls in love with Hero, not quite at first sight, as he claims to have seen her before the war. However then, having other matters on his mind, he did not 'drive liking to the name of love' *(Act 1, Scene 1)*. On seeing her again after the war, he is immediately taken with her, despite knowing little about her (he has to ask Don Pedro if Leonato has any other children). Moments after this meeting, he plans to make her his wife.

Shakespeare emphasizes Claudio's youthfulness and inexperience. Claudio seeks reassurance from his friends about his choice of wife and doesn't trust his ability to speak for himself, allowing the Prince to woo for him. After behaving peevishly at the party, thinking that Don Pedro has misled him, he then reacts to the news of the successful engagement with Hero with silence, causing Beatrice to prompt him 'Speak, Count, 'tis your cue.' *(Act 2, Scene 1)* Perhaps befitting his role as a soldier, Claudio is more confident conversing with his male companions, inventively contributing to Benedick's 'gulling' and his subsequent teasing. His dialogue with Hero is very limited, indicating what he calls 'Bashful sincerity and comely love' *(Act 4, Scene 1)*. However, he is at his most articulate and poetic in his public denunciation of Hero in the church.

The cruelty of his jealous actions requires him to undergo a **penitential** act in Act 5, Scene 3, in which he admits his guilt and seeks forgiveness, which leads to his **redemption**. His reward is the desired happy ending in which he marries Hero.

Key quotations

I look'd upon her with a soldier's eye,
That lik'd, but had a rougher task in hand
Than to drive liking to the name of love. *(Claudio, Act 1, Scene 1)*

There, Leonato, take her back again.
Give not this rotten orange to your friend! *(Claudio, Act 4, Scene 1)*

Activity 8

1. To what extent is Claudio a sympathetic character? Claudio is praised by many characters in the play and described as **'doing in the figure of a lamb the feats of a lion'** yet he behaves cruelly towards Hero in Act 4 and heartlessly towards Leonato in Act 5, Scene 1. Write a paragraph exploring the positive and negative aspects of Claudio's character.

2. Imagine you are a casting director who has been asked to find the perfect actor for the role of Claudio. Bring in three pictures of possible candidates for the part and explain what aspects of the character they could represent well.

Hero

Hero is a character who is admired for her modesty, sweetness and beauty, and is considered 'worthy' of the love of a count. An obedient daughter, she agrees to marry whomever her father chooses for her, and seems very pleased with her **'dear Claudio'**. However, she experiences some foreboding on the morning of the wedding, as she says her **'heart is exceeding heavy'** *(Act 3, Scene 4)*. Her fears come true when she is humiliated at the church and she is unable to explain why a man was seen speaking at her window.

Although she can been seen as a frustratingly passive character (she and Claudio have been described by a critic as 'mild and immature young lovers'), she is playful and clever when mocking Beatrice in Act 3, Scene 1.

penitential expressing regret or requesting forgiveness for wrongdoing

redemption being forgiven for sin, atoning for a mistake or fault

Key quotations

I will do any modest office, my lord, to help my cousin to a good husband. *(Hero, Act 2, Scene 1)*

If I know more of any man alive
Than that which maiden modesty doth warrant,
Let all my sins lack mercy. *(Hero, Act 4, Scene 1)*

Hero is a dutiful daughter, as shown in the RSC production that was part of the 2012 World Shakespeare Festival

Activity 9

Hero can seem a less interesting character than her vibrant cousin, Beatrice. However, Elizabethan audiences would have perceived her as the more conventional young woman in a courting relationship. Write a paragraph comparing and contrasting Hero and Claudio's dialogue with that of Benedick and Beatrice.

Activity 10

Hero is a Greek name, well known because of the myth of Hero and Leander. Hero, a priestess of Aphrodite, the goddess of love, lived in a tower and her lover Leander, guided by a light from her tower, would swim the **Hellespont** to be with her. One night, the light blew out and Leander drowned. In grief, Hero threw herself out of tower and died. (Benedick mentions this myth in Act 5, Scene 2: **'Leander the good swimmer… never so truly turned over and over as my poor self in love.'**) With a partner, discuss why you think Shakespeare has given this name to Hero.

Don John

Don John, also described as 'the Bastard', is the illegitimate brother of Don Pedro. In Elizabethan society, illegitimate children were seen as upsetting the order of society. They were unlikely to inherit and, in some cases, had to rely on the generosity of their 'legitimate' relations. Shakespeare explores the role of 'bastard' children in several plays, most famously with the evil, scheming Edmund in *King Lear*, who defiantly exclaims, 'Now, gods, stand up for bastards.' Don John is another representative of these uncomfortable outsiders. Though virtually silent in his first scene, Don John reveals his malicious intentions against his brother and Claudio in Act 1, Scene 3. He is a **malcontent** who seems to gain enjoyment only through causing pain to others (**'if I had my mouth I would bite'**) and declares himself a **'plain-dealing villain'** (*Act 1, Scene 3*). Despite saying he **'cannot hide'** what he is (*Act 3, Scene 2*), he **dissembles** well enough to convince his brother and Claudio that Hero is unfaithful.

Activity 11

1. Don John and Don Pedro obviously have a troubled relationship. Closely read Act 1, Scene 3 and write bullet points on why Don John wants to cause mischief for Don Pedro.

2. What would a doctor say? Working with a partner, one of you should play a psychiatrist while the other plays Don John. The 'psychiatrist' should ask 'Don John' probing questions about his feelings of discontent and inferiority. Afterwards, make bullet points of all the possible reasons for Don John's behaviour.

Key quotations

You have of late stood out against your brother, and he hath ta'en you newly into his grace, where it is impossible you should take true root but by the fair weather that you make yourself. *(Conrad, Act 1, Scene 3)*

Tips for assessment

In your assessment, remember to write about the characters as constructions of the playwright, not real people. Use phrases like 'Shakespeare presents…' or 'In this scene, the playwright shows…'.

Dogberry

Dogberry is the local constable. In Elizabethan times, constables were used to keep order, but it was not a desirable position and they wielded little power. Therefore most constables came from the poorer and less educated classes, and they rarely stayed in their jobs for long. Shakespeare has comic constables in other plays, including Dull in *Love's Labours Lost* and Elbow in *Measure for Measure*. We know that the comic actor William Kempe originally played Dogberry, as his name, or an abbreviation of it, appeared on some of Dogberry's speeches in the First Folio.

In Act 3, Scene 3 the lack of power of the constables is comically presented, as Dogberry advises the watch to 'take no note' of those who disobey them, to 'make no noise' and that he cannot see 'how [their] sleeping should offend'. Although Dogberry, with his self-importance (is he really as rich, wise and 'pretty a piece of flesh' as he claims in Act 4, Scene 2?) and mangled dialogue, is clearly a comic character, he also represents a well-intentioned, simple local figure. In Act 3, Scene 5, Leonato greets him as 'honest neighbour' and had Leonato only understood the importance of what Dogberry was trying to convey, then the unhappy scene at the church could have been averted.

Although *Much Ado About Nothing* is a comedy, there are scenes of tension as well. One of Dogberry's dramatic functions is to provide **comic relief**. For example, he is first introduced in Act 3, Scene 3, after the initial accusation against Hero in the previous scene, and the near-tragic events of Act 4, Scene 1 are followed by Dogberry's humorous questioning of the prisoners, reminding the audience that they are watching a comedy.

Key quotations

O that he were here to write me down an ass! But, masters, remember that I am an ass. Though it be not written down, yet forget not that I am an ass. *(Dogberry, Act 4, Scene 2)*

---

comic relief amusing scenes which provide a temporary release of tension

dissemble give a false appearance

Hellespont a narrow strait in Turkey, important in Greek mythology and now called the Dardanelles

malcontent a dissatisfied person, possibly one who feels grievances due to thwarted ambitions or unhappiness with the established social order

Activity 12

William Kempe, one of the most famous and popular comic actors of the Elizabethan age, was the first Dogberry. He was known for dancing, physical comedy and improvising. In a small group, closely read Act 4, Scene 2 and consider how many ways you could use physical comedy to intensify the comic effect of this scene.

Will Kempe dances with bells on his legs, accompanied by pipe and tabor

Minor characters

Borachio

Borachio is a follower of Don John and lover of Margaret. He overhears the conversation between the Prince and Claudio, providing the ammunition for the first piece of mischief. Then, in Act 2, Scene 2, he devises the complicated plot to discredit Hero. It may be his tendency to drink (his name derives from the Spanish word *barracho*, meaning drunkard or wine bottle) that causes him to reveal the plot on a public street, leading to Conrad and him being arrested by the 'shallow fools', the Watch in Act 5, Scene 1. He seems genuinely repentant. He absolves Margaret of any role in the plot, saying she 'hath been just and virtuous' and asks for 'nothing but the reward of a villain' (Act 5, Scene 1).

Activity 13

Shakespeare does not present the scene in which Borachio is wooing Margaret at Hero's chamber on stage. Write down what that scene might have contained and discuss why Shakespeare chose to show only the aftermath of the scene.

Activity 14

In Act 3, Scene 3, Borachio says that he will tell the plot to Conrad **'like a true drunkard'**. This may simply mean that those who are drunk often tell the truth or it may allude to Borachio's actual physical state, given his name and his indiscretion. Try playing this scene in two ways, one in which Borachio is sober and the other when he is inebriated. Which do you think works best and why?

Conrad

Conrad is Don John's companion and follower, in whom he confides his innermost thoughts. Some recent productions of the play have emphasized the closeness between the characters by suggesting that Conrad is Don John's lover, and, in the 2012 film version of *Much Ado About Nothing*, the director Joss Whedon cast a beautiful woman in the role. Conrad listens to and advises Don John, is arrested with Borachio after hearing about the plot to deceive Claudio and, in Act 4, Scene 2, memorably calls Dogberry 'an ass'.

Activity 15

Conrad says he will assist Don John **'to the death'** *(Act 1, Scene 3)*. With a partner, take turns on the 'hot seat'. One of you plays Conrad while the other asks questions to determine why Conrad is so loyal. Consider what Don John might achieve, how Conrad might benefit from helping him and what their relationship is.

Tips for assessment

It is important to consider the different ways a character could be interpreted. Understanding how an actor could portray a character's motivations is one way of considering interpretation.

Margaret

Margaret is one of two gentlewomen who serve Hero. She is a lively character, quick to imagine sexual **innuendo** in her playful conversations with others. She flirtatiously asks Benedick to **'write me a sonnet in praise of my beauty'** *(Act 5, Scene 2)* and teases Hero before her wedding with **'Twill be heavier soon by the weight of a man'** *(Act 3, Scene 4)*. Although Borachio says that she was unaware of the implications of her dressing up as Hero, by agreeing to do so, she was instrumental in his plot's success. Yet her scenes following this event display no sign of guilt and she is not seen to be punished for her actions.

innuendo a hint or hidden reference to something rude, often sexual

Ursula

Ursula is Hero's other gentlewoman and plays an important role in Act 3, Scene 1 when she and Hero trick Beatrice. She shows deference to Hero, for example, by calling her 'madam' but is also clearly trusted enough by Hero to be included in this intrigue.

Activity 16

As both Ursula and Margaret are simply described as gentlewomen, it is easy to think that they are indistinguishable. However, the characters are clearly distinguished by Shakespeare. Create a chart like the one below to draw conclusions about the differences between the characters.

Act, Scene	Margaret's actions and/or dialogue	What this means	Ursula's actions and/or dialogue	What this means
Act 2, Scene 1	Balthasar pursues her. She says she has 'many ill qualities'.		She teases Antonio about being old: 'waggling of your head', 'dry hand'.	
Act 3, Scene 1	She goes to fetch Beatrice.		She helps Hero to fool Beatrice: 'So angle we for Beatrice…'.	
Act 3, Scene 4	She helps Hero to dress and teases her about her wedding night. She also taunts Beatrice about Benedick.		She is sent to wake Beatrice.	
Act 5, Scene 2	She has a playful scene with Benedick about love and wit, and then is sent to call Beatrice.		She arrives at the end of the scene to say that it is 'proved' that Hero is innocent.	

Antonio

Antonio is Leonato's brother. He is described as 'old' in some stage directions and this is reinforced by Ursula's teasing him about his 'waggling' head and 'dry' hands in Act 2, Scene 1. Most of his scenes are with Leonato whom he loyally supports in Act 5, Scene 1. Claudio refers to the altercation with Leonato and Antonio as 'We had liked to have had our noses snapped off with two old men without teeth.' *(Act 5, Scene 1)*. He is also present in the final scene when he sums up the happy ending saying, 'Well, I am glad that all things sorts so well.' *(Act 5, Scene 4)*

Activity 17

Write a paragraph comparing the relationship between the two pairs of brothers in the play: Antonio and Leonato, and Don John and Don Pedro.

Friar Francis

Although England was a Protestant country at this time, Shakespeare has set the play in the Catholic country of Italy. A friar was a member of a Roman Catholic order. Like Friar Lawrence in *Romeo and Juliet*, Friar Francis suggests a solution to a dilemma for a young bride-to-be.

Friar Francis only appears in the two wedding scenes (Act 4, Scene 1 and Act 5, Scene 4) but is important to the play's outcome as he suggests the plan to save Hero's honour. To this extent, he could be said to provide the **deus ex machina** as his extraordinary role in pretending that Hero is dead saves what appears to be a hopeless situation.

Balthasar

Balthasar is an attendant of Don Pedro's mainly memorable for being the musician in the play. In Act 2, Scene 3, he sings a song about the deceitfulness of men, 'Men were deceivers ever', which is ironic as Claudio and Don Pedro then deceive Benedick into thinking Beatrice has declared her love for him. In Act 5, Scene 3, he sings a song in Hero's tomb, asking for forgiveness: 'Pardon, goddess of the night…'.

Activity 18

Balthasar is not the only singer in the play. In Act 5, Scene 2, Benedick tries to sing a song, but interrupts himself. Write a paragraph explaining the different dramatic effects of Balthasar's songs and Benedick's.

Verges

Verges is the Headborough or second-in-command constable and works closely with Dogberry, whom he seems to admire.

> **deus ex machina** a surprising and unlikely plot device which brings about a resolution to what seemed to be an impossible situation

The Watch

The Watch are the group of local men, 'good and true' *(Act 3, Scene 3)*, who have been gathered together to conduct that night's patrol. They seem to be very inexperienced as they ask basic questions (and receive confusing responses from Dogberry). In the script, they are not differentiated and lines are simply attributed to 'A Watchman', but we know the names of the two who can write and read: Hugh Oatcake and George Seacoal. Despite their simple natures and limited training, they successfully arrest Borachio and Conrad.

Key quotations

Never speak, we charge you. Let us obey you to go with us.
(A Watchman, Act 3, Scene 3)

Activity 19

Closely read the section from Act 3, Scene 3 when the Watch arrest Borachio and Conrad, beginning 'We charge you in the prince's name. Stand!' Write a series of director's notes suggesting how this scene could be staged to maximize its comic and dramatic potential.

The Sexton

A sexton was an assistant to a parish clerk and the character is used in Act 4, Scene 2 to provide the voice of reason, playing 'straight man' to the comic duo of Dogberry and Verges. He takes notes on the testimony and attempts to guide Dogberry in the rudiments of court examinations. Eventually he takes over the interrogation himself and connects the overheard conversation with Hero's disgrace and Don John's escape.

Writing about character

Upgrade

In your assessment, you will need to demonstrate your understanding of the characters, whether or not the question specifically names them. You may need to consider how the characters are revealed through the language they use, their connection to the play's themes or their importance to its plot. Remember that you are not writing about actual people but characters that Shakespeare has moulded and presented in a specific way. The characters can be interpreted in many different ways depending on the choices of the directors, designers and actors involved.

You should consider:

- how the characters reveal themselves through the language they use

- when a specific character is introduced in the play and what other characters say about him or her

- if there are any hints about the character's physical appearance or actions

- whether the character changes and develops throughout the course of the play

- If the character is well rounded and believable or if he or she is a more two-dimensional stock character

- what the character's specific dramatic function is in the play (e.g. to provide comic relief or to bring about the downfall of another character)

- whether Shakespeare creates sympathy for the character

- if you can make any points about this character's relationship with another character (such as the relationship between brothers or comic duo potential)

- whether you can contrast this character with another character in the play (e.g. Beatrice with Hero, or Claudio with Benedick).

Character map

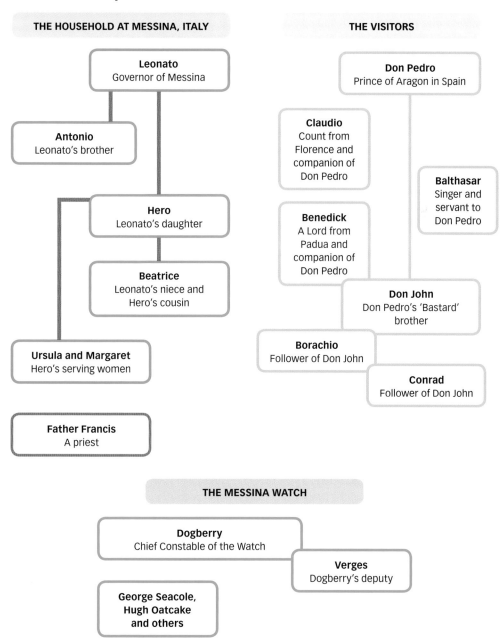

THE HOUSEHOLD AT MESSINA, ITALY

Leonato
Governor of Messina

Antonio
Leonato's brother

Hero
Leonato's daughter

Beatrice
Leonato's niece and
Hero's cousin

Ursula and Margaret
Hero's serving women

Father Francis
A priest

THE VISITORS

Don Pedro
Prince of Aragon in Spain

Claudio
Count from
Florence and
companion of
Don Pedro

Balthasar
Singer and
servant to
Don Pedro

Benedick
A Lord from
Padua and
companion of
Don Pedro

Don John
Don Pedro's 'Bastard'
brother

Borachio
Follower of Don John

Conrad
Follower of Don John

THE MESSINA WATCH

Dogberry
Chief Constable of the Watch

Verges
Dogberry's deputy

**George Seacole,
Hugh Oatcake
and others**

Language

In many ways, *Much Ado About Nothing* is a play about language. There are characters who speak too much and others who are too silent; characters who speak skilfully and others far too clumsily; characters who speak falsely and others truthfully. Words are proven to be exciting and dangerous, with Benedick ultimately stopping Beatrice's flow of verbal wit with a kiss, 'Peace, I will stop your mouth', in order to bring them together *(Act 5, Scene 4)*.

Verse and prose

Shakespeare is associated with verse, particularly **blank verse**, which contains unrhymed lines with a regular metre. In Elizabethan drama, this is usually **iambic pentameter**, which consists of lines of ten beats or syllables with the stress on the even beats (2, 4, 6, 8, 10).

> ### Activity 1
>
> 1. Write out and mark up the following lines from Act 4, Scene 1 to show which beats are stressed.
>
>   'O Hero! What a Hero hadst though been
>   If half thy outward graces had been plac'd
>   About thy thoughts and counsels of thy heart!'
>
> 2. Practise saying these lines stressing those beats.

There are relatively few examples of rhyming verse in the play. A notable example is Hero's use of a **rhyming couplet** before exiting Act 3, Scene 1, followed by Beatrice's ten alternating rhyming lines, which end the scene. Hero's couplet, spoken in an **aside** to the audience, neatly finishes off her 'gulling' plot, while Beatrice's lines bring a heightened romance in an unfinished sonnet.

Verse is used in key moments of *Much Ado About Nothing*, but an unusual amount of the play is written in **prose**. Whereas 90% of *Romeo and Juliet* is written in verse and 80% of *A Midsummer Night's Dream*, only 30% of *Much Ado About Nothing* is in verse. Traditionally, Shakespeare used prose more when writing lower-class characters or when characters are in more informal and comic situations, but 70% of the lines in *Much Ado About Nothing* are in prose, including much of the dialogue between the upper-class characters, such as the witty **repartee** between Benedick and Beatrice.

It is interesting to note when characters switch from prose to verse. While it is not surprising that Dogberry's comic scenes are written in prose, the pattern of other scenes is less predictable. For example, in Act 1, Scene 1, the dialogue is in prose until Claudio confesses his love of Hero to Don Pedro, when he switches to verse:

> 'Your liege, your highness now may do me good.'

Benedick's 'gulling' scene (Act 2, Scene 3) is in prose, but Beatrice's 'gulling' scene (Act 3, Scene 1) is in blank verse. Most of Act 4, Scene 1 is in verse, but when Beatrice and Benedick are left alone, they speak in prose. Claudio's repentance is formal rhyming verse, whereas in the previous prose scene, Benedick declares, 'I was not born under a rhyming planet, nor cannot woo in festival terms' (Act 5, Scene 2). Shakespeare may be making a point about the untrustworthiness of Claudio's conventional verse compared with the down-to-earth prose of Benedick's love.

However, it would be wrong to think that this means the prose spoken is ordinary conversation. Instead, the language is ripe with **imagery**, rhetoric and wordplay.

Imagery

The play is rich in figurative language and below are some of the common images that occur.

War and weapons

In a play in which the leading male characters are returning soldiers and there is a battle of wits between reluctant lovers, it is not surprising that much of the imagery deals with conflict. In the first scene, Leonato tells the messenger of the 'merry war' between Benedick and Beatrice leading to a 'skirmish of wit between them'. This is reinforced by Benedick in Act 2, Scene 1 when he compares Beatrice's jibes to 'stabs'. In Act 2, Scene 3, war **metaphors** are used to describe Beatrice's supposed battle to control her love for Benedick: '... wisdom and blood combating in so tender a body, we have ten proofs to one that blood hath the victory'. Love and violence follow closely upon each other when Beatrice's declaration of love for Benedick in Act 4, Scene 1 is followed immediately by 'Kill Claudio.' In the final scene of the play Benedick and Claudio resume their friendship, but with words that suggest conflict: 'beaten thee', 'cudgelled thee'.

aside when a character speaks directly to the audience, unheard by the other characters on stage

blank verse unrhymed lines of poetry with a regular metre

iambic pentameter a line of verse with ten syllables, forming five 'feet' where the stress falls on the second syllable of each foot, e.g. 'Up-on the in-stant that she was a-ccus'd'

imagery the use of visual or other vivid language to convey ideas or emotions

metaphor a figure of speech applied to something to suggest a resemblance, without using the words 'like' or 'as'

prose any writing in continuous form without rhythm or rhyme

repartee conversation characterized by witty replies

rhyming couplet two consecutive lines that rhyme

Nature and disease

The two 'gulling' scenes provide examples of Shakespeare's use of nature imagery. In Act 2, Scene 3, the tricksters imagine themselves to be hunters, encouraging each other to 'stalk on' while 'the fowl' (in this case, Benedick) 'sits' waiting to be shot. Later, Claudio changes the metaphor to fishing: 'Bait the hook well. This fish will bite.' *(Act 2, Scene 3)* Ursula and Hero use similar nature imagery in the following scene. Both of these scenes take place in the orchard and this heightens the use of imagery derived from their surroundings.

Regent's Park in London provided a natural backdrop for the orchard scene in this Open Air Theatre production in 2009

Nature imagery can have negative **connotations**. Don John prefers to be a 'canker in a hedge' *(Act 1, Scene 3)* and Claudio uses the metaphor 'rotten orange' to describe Hero *(Act 4, Scene 1)*. In his denunciation of Hero, Claudio uses a **simile** to contrast what he believed Hero to be, 'As chaste as is the bud ere it be blown' to what he believes he has discovered, that she is an animal who rages in 'savage sensuality' *(Act 4, Scene 1)*. Infection and plague are also mentioned in the play, showing that nature can be corrupted.

> **connotation** association with a word beyond its literal meaning
>
> **simile** a comparison between two things using the word 'like' or 'as'

Activity 2

Carefully read Act 3, Scene 1 from Beatrice's entrance to Hero and Ursula's exit.

1. Identify all the nature imagery you can discover in that scene.

2. Write a paragraph explaining the effect the use of nature imagery has.

Cuckolds

The fear of infidelity runs throughout the play and is reflected in the language used. Don John is, of course, the illegitimate brother of Don Pedro, and Hero is accused of unfaithfulness. In Act 1, Scene 1, when Don Pedro asks if Hero is Leonato's daughter, Leonato replies **'Her mother hath many times told me so'** hinting at the lack of certainty (in the days before paternity tests) that a husband might feel.

In Elizabethan times, men whose wives were unfaithful to them were called **cuckolds** and were said to sprout horns upon their heads. One of Benedick's arguments against marriage is that he would become a cuckold: **'... but if ever the sensible Benedick bear it, pluck off the bull's horns and set them in my forehead... 'Here you may see Benedick, the married man.''** *(Act 1, Scene 1)* Horn imagery continues throughout the play, though in the end, Benedick seems to accept it more joyously, proclaiming to the Prince, **'There is no staff more reverend than one tipped in horn.'** *(Act 5, Scene 4)*

Music

Some critics observe that the 'nothing' in the title could also refer to 'notes' of music. When asked to play a song for Don Pedro, Balthasar makes a **pun**:

> **Note this before my notes:**
> **There's not a note of mine that's worth noting.'** *(Act 2, Scene 3)*

Benedick compares the change in Claudio from being the soldier with **'no music with him but the drum and the fife'** (military music) to being transformed into a lover who prefers **'the tabor and the pipe'** (music for dancing) *(Act 2, Scene 3)*. Beatrice too compares the progress of love to different types of music: wooing is a **'hot and hasty'** jig, the wedding is done in a more mannerly measure and then the repentance is a desperate **'cinquepace'** *(Act 2, Scene 1)*.

> **cuckold** a husband whose wife was unfaithful to him; a term of insult to a man, suggesting he was weak and impotent
>
> **pun** a joke that relies on double meaning or similar sounds of words

Tips for assessment

When writing about language in your assessment, make sure you use the correct terminology, such as 'metaphor', 'verse' or 'pun'. However, don't just note these techniques, but also explain the effect that is created by their use.

Mythology and the Bible

Shakespeare moves freely between ancient Greek and Roman mythology and biblical **allusions** throughout the play. Unsurprisingly, the most frequently mentioned classical figure is Cupid, the playful god of love and desire who wielded a bow and arrow to cause unsuspecting people to fall in love. Beatrice claims that Benedick 'challenged Cupid' to prove who was better at making people fall in love *(Act 1, Scene 1)* and Don Pedro also believes he can do a better job when he plans to trick Benedick and Beatrice into falling in love: 'Cupid is no longer an archer; his glory shall be ours' *(Act 2, Scene 1)*. Also mentioned are Hercules, known for his strength and bravery; Ate, the Greek goddess of mischief and discord; and Europa, a Phoenician woman in Greek mythology who was abducted by a god in the form of a bull.

Biblical references include Adam, the first man, aspects of creation and Saint Peter at heaven's gate.

Activity 3

Read the following classical or biblical allusions from the play and then write an analysis of what you think each means.

1. **'So deliver I up my apes, and away to Saint Peter fore the heavens. He shows me where the bachelors sit, and there live we as merry as the day is long.'**
   (Beatrice, Act 2, Scene 1)

2. **'Adam's sons are my brethren, and truly I hold it a sin to match in my kindred.'**
   (Beatrice, Act 2, Scene 1)

3. **'Of this matter / Is little Cupid's crafty arrow made / That only wounds by hearsay.'**
   (Hero, Act 3, Scene 1)

4. **'He hath twice or thrice cut Cupid's bowstring, and the little hangman dare not shoot at him.'**
   (Don Pedro, Act 3, Scene 2)

5. **'He is now as valiant as Hercules that only tells a lie and swears it.'**
   (Beatrice, Act 4, Scene 1)

6. **'As once Europa did at lusty Jove / When he would play the noble beast in love.'**
   (Claudio, Act 5, Scene 4)

allusion a mention or reference to something, such as a familiar story or classic text

Other language techniques

Personification

One technique which Shakespeare uses freely in *Much Ado About Nothing* is **personification**, which makes the dialogue more vivid and lively. Beatrice becomes the walking embodiment of scorn when she is called 'Lady Disdain' in the first scene. Claudio emphasizes his impatience to be married with the personification 'Time goes on crutches till love have all his rites' *(Act 2, Scene 1)*. Personification is often used to make abstract concepts real, but also to add a dramatic, sometimes exaggerated, quality to the speech.

Rhetoric, antithesis and repetition

Shakespeare is believed to have studied rhetoric at school. The ability to understand and construct arguments was considered an essential skill in order to participate in many aspects of Elizabethan life, such as public debates or writing letters. Techniques such as **antithesis** and **repetition**, as well as the ability to structure them to create maximum impact, would have been valued rhetorical skills.

These same techniques can be appreciated in the speech of Shakespeare's characters. To emphasize the truth of what he says, Claudio issues a series of **rhetorical questions**, e.g. 'Leonato, stand I here?' *(Act 4, Scene 1)*.

antithesis either starting a sentence with a proposition to which the opposite is then presented or when two opposites are put together for contrasting effect , e.g. 'Come, lady, die to live' *(Act 4, Scene 1)*

personification when human qualities are attributed to something non-human such as an object or an idea

repetition repeating of a word in a sentence or speech

rhetorical question a question asked for effect rather than expecting an answer

Claudio denounces Hero using antithesis to highlight the contrast between her appearance and what he believes to be the reality, juxtaposing her 'show of truth' with her 'cunning sin' *(Act 4, Scene 1)*. When departing from her, he says:

But fare thee well, most foul, most fair; farewell
Thou pure impiety and impious purity. *(Act 4, Scene 1)*

This use of **oxymorons** heightens the sense of Claudio's conflicting emotions towards Hero and her apparent contradictions.

Repetition is also used to create rhetorical effects. Don John damns Hero with the devastating repetition of her name, 'Even she – Leonato's Hero, your Hero, every man's Hero', conjuring a Hero who has kept the company of many men *(Act 3, Scene 1)*. In Act 4, Scene 1, Claudio repeats this critical repetition of her name, 'Marry, that can Hero. / Hero itself can blot out Hero's virtue' and 'O Hero! What a Hero hadst thou been…', contrasting the heroic nature of her name with her alleged low behaviour.

Activity 6

Repetition is used for comic effect as well. Look at Act 4, Scene 2 from Conrad's line 'Away, you are an ass; you are an ass' to the end. Note the number of times 'ass' is said and consider how this could add to the comic effect of this scene.

Wordplay

'The exuberant quality of lively minds which strike fire by scoring off each other: the quality I called competitive vitality…' A.P. Rossiter in *Angels with Horns*

Benedick and Beatrice, in particular, but also many of the other inhabitants of Messina have what the critic A.P. Rossiter calls 'dancing minds' and 'make words dance to their unpremeditated tunes'. They engage in comic wordplay, which highlights their wit, but also the conflict between them.

One type of wordplay uses a word with more than one meaning in a way to indicate an understanding of both meanings. For example, in Act 1, Scene 1, when Beatrice refers to Benedick as having 'an excellent stomach', she could mean that he was courageous or, more insultingly, that he was greedy. Similarly, 'stuffed' can mean 'full of', which is what the messenger means when he says Benedick is 'stuffed with all honourable virtues' *(Act 1, Scene 1)*. However, a 'stuffed man' is a scarecrow, which is the insult Beatrice derives from this. In Act 3, Scene 4, Beatrice says that she is full of cold: 'I am stuffed, cousin; I cannot smell', but Margaret quickly suggests a sexual innuendo in her reply, 'A maid, and stuffed!'.

oxymoron a figure of speech that contains apparently contradictory ideas

Beatrice plays with the sounds of words. In Act 2, Scene 1, she refers to Claudio as being 'civil as an orange', making a pun on the word 'Seville', a city famous for providing bitter oranges. So instead of simply meaning that Claudio is polite as 'civil' would suggest, she is implying that he is sour like a bitter fruit.

Benedick is particularly fond of **hyperbole**, which accords with his self-dramatizing personality: **'I will go on the slightest errand now to the Antipodes … rather than hold three words' conference with this harpy.'** *(Act 2, Scene 1)*

Benedick and Beatrice spar with words, in the RSC production in 1996

Activity 7

1. Look closely at the first 'skirmish of wit' between Benedick and Beatrice in Act 1, Scene 1 from **'I wonder that you will still be talking…'** to **'You always end with a jade's trick. I know you of old.'** Identify any examples of the following language techniques:

   - personification (e.g. 'disdain should die…')
   - antithesis
   - hyperbole
   - metaphor
   - insults.

2. Write a paragraph explaining what we learn about these characters and their relationship through their use of language.

hyperbole use of exaggeration

Malapropisms

Dogberry, and some of the members of the Watch, use **malapropisms** where they substitute a word that sounds similar to the word they mean, but which has a different or even opposite meaning. Verges and Dogberry begin their interview with the Watch by saying that if they aren't good and true they should 'suffer salvation' when they mean 'damnation'. Instead of trying to find the most deserving men, they ask for the most 'desertless'. (Act 3, Scene 3)

The Watch instruct the culprits they are arresting them to 'let us obey you' when they mean to command (Act 3, Scene 3). Dogberry's malapropisms cause so much confusion that Leonato cannot take him seriously when he comes to speak to him about a matter which 'descerns' (he means 'concerns') him (Act 3, Scene 5).

Activity 8

In the chart below are some words that Dogberry, Verges or the Watch misuse. Find where the word occurs in the text, and then write down what you believe the correct word should be.

Malapropism	Who says it and when	Correct Word
Dissembly		
Redemption		
Opinioned		
Excommunication		
Auspicious		

malapropism using an incorrect word for another, often creating a comic effect

Writing about language

Upgrade

It is very important when writing about *Much Ado About Nothing* that you demonstrate that you understand the language of the play. Even if you don't believe that the question is specifically asking you about language, you need to show how Shakespeare has created certain effects or differentiated characters by the language used.

In order to prepare for this, practise doing the following:

- Write about the play as a play, not a novel or a story.

- Pick out short quotations to support your points.

- Revise the literary terminology defined in this chapter and try to discover at least one example of that technique beyond the ones already provided.

- Use literary terminology correctly, looking out for metaphors, allusions, rhymes and hyperbole. However, don't just note these techniques but also explain the effect that is created by their use.

- Consider the way different characters use language, e.g. Beatrice as opposed to Dogberry.

- Note whether a passage is in verse or prose, and try to decide why Shakespeare made that choice.

- Explore the different ways a line could be interpreted.

Themes

The themes of the play, including its depiction of the battle of the sexes, love and jealousy, have been at the heart of its appeal for audiences over the years. As you read the play, note when you think a key theme is being highlighted. When you see a production of the play, consider how the director interpreted particular themes such as the portrayal of gender roles or status.

Love

'Wooing, wedding, wiving' are said by the critic A.P. Rossiter to be the key topics of the play, and love in its many forms is central to the plot. The wooing of Hero is introduced in the first scene and the play ends with the wedding and wiving of Benedick and Beatrice, and Claudio and Hero. In between these scenes, many different aspects of love are portrayed.

There is the conventional young romantic love that Claudio feels for Hero, the complicated love that Benedick and Beatrice experience, and the parental love Leonato expresses for his daughter. In each of these cases, there is an **impediment** to the love, which causes conflict. In some cases, the obstacle to love is based on aspects of the characters, such as their pride or gullibility, while sometimes the conflict is caused by an external force such as false accusations. Often, there is a combination of both internal and external factors.

Activity 1

Create a chart like the one below to help you analyse how different types of love are presented in the play.

Type of love	Characters involved	Impediment to love	Key quotations
	Hero and Claudio		
	Beatrice and Benedick		
	Leonato and Hero		

impediment an obstacle or barrier

The battle of the sexes

Key to the play's attraction for audiences and performers is its depiction of the battle between the sexes. If Beatrice and Benedick were not such equal and appealing combatants, much of the play's humour and excitement would be lost. The exploration of gender roles is reinforced by the structure of the play. The male 'gulling' scene of Act 2, Scene 3 is followed immediately by its parallel female version in Act 3, Scene 1. Throughout the play, the idea of male/female pairings is reinforced, particularly in Act 2, Scene 1, when a series of couples are seen flirting, wooing, teasing and arguing.

Both Beatrice and Benedick have speeches in which they explain why no member of the opposite sex will ever suit them. In Act 1, Scene 1, Benedick declares, 'Because I will not do them the wrong to mistrust any, I will do myself the right to trust none... I will live a bachelor', while in Act 3, Scene 2, Beatrice says she could not 'endure a husband with a beard', nor one without a beard ('I am not for him' *(Act 2, Scene 1)* so is determined to go to heaven 'where the bachelors sit' *(Act 2, Scene 1)*. Both stress the apparent impossibility of a peaceful relationship with anyone of the opposite sex.

Beatrice is a character who pushes against the boundaries of what can be expected of a woman in her society. In Act 4, Scene 1, out of frustration, she exclaims 'O that I were a man for his sake!' when she longs to avenge Hero, but then mourns 'I cannot be a man with wishing; therefore I will die a woman with grieving.' Benedick takes on the 'man's office' of challenging Claudio (Act 4, Scene 1), but also comically shows his softer side in his attempts to write poetry in honour of Beatrice. Their mutual strength and desire to outdo one another is summed up by Benedick when he says, 'Thou and I are too wise to woo peaceably.' *(Act 5, Scene 2)*

There is also evidence of a double standard in terms of how the women and men are expected to behave in society. Benedick seems to have a reputation as something of a lady's man (e.g. Leonato jokingly says that Hero must be his legitimate daughter because Benedick was only a child when she was conceived) and Benedick boasts that he is 'loved of all ladies' except for Beatrice *(Act 1, Scene 1)*. However, the possibility of Hero being anything other than a modest 'maid' is a terrible scandal.

Tips for assessment

Upgrade

When writing about themes, try to discover how the theme is developed throughout the play, rather than writing about a single example.

Activity 2

Compare the behaviour of the female characters in the play with that of the male characters. For example, compare Act 3, Scene 4 when the women are helping Hero to prepare for her wedding with the men's behaviour in Act 5, Scene 1. You should consider:

- the location of the scenes
- what actions and movements are suggested by the dialogue
- the type of language used
- any similarities and differences between the male and female characters.

Activity 3

At the beginning of Act 2, Scene 3, Benedick has a soliloquy in which he expresses his feelings about love and women. In your own words, write down how he feels love has changed Claudio. Then write a paragraph summing up why Benedick is so against love and marriage.

Friendship

One of the choices Benedick makes is between his love for Beatrice and his friendship with Claudio and Don Pedro. At first he seems to be a character who, although possibly experienced in love, is most comfortable in the company of men. Beatrice, however, casts some doubt over the depth of Benedick's friendships, claiming **'He hath every month a new sworn brother.'** *(Act 1, Scene 1)* Claudio also behaves differently when with his soldier friends. In the early scenes, he is tongue-tied in Hero's presence and yet confident and talkative with the male characters.

Both Don Pedro and Don John have followers, characters whose status is lower than theirs but to whom they are close. Claudio gains status through Don Pedro's having **'bestowed much honour'** on him *(Act 1, Scene 1)* and, in an act of friendship, Don Pedro offers to woo Hero on Claudio's behalf, confident that he can win her for his friend. Conrad is described as Don John's companion and it is in his company that Don John is able to express fully his complaints and desires. Although Conrad is subservient to Don John (and calls him **'my lord'**), he also has the confidence to give him advice (**'you should hear reason'**) *(Act 1, Scene 3)*. However, Conrad isn't successful in moderating Don John's behaviour and his other follower, Borachio actively encourages Don John's plotting.

Beatrice remains steadfastly loyal to Hero, as shown in the RSC production in 1996

The friendship between Hero and Beatrice is one of the strongest and most consistent bonds in the play. Beatrice's support of Hero is unwavering and her demand for vengeance causes Benedick to choose between his love for Beatrice and his good friends. At first, this demand seems as if it will cause a new obstacle in Benedick and Beatrice's romance. The end of the play suggests that the friendships between the men have been repaired, with Benedick's exhortation, 'Come, come we are friends.' *(Act 5, Scene 4)*

Activity 4

In Act 4, Benedick must make a choice between siding with Claudio and Don Pedro, or defending Hero at Beatrice's request. Use the quotations below from Act 4 and Act 5 as the starting point for a paragraph in which you discuss where Benedick's loyalties lie.

Yet, by my honour, I will deal in this
As secretly and justly as your soul
Should with your body. *(Benedick, Act 4, Scene 1)*

Beatrice: **Kill Claudio.**
Benedick: **Ha! Not for the wide world.** *(Act 4, Scene 1)*

Think you in your soul the Count Claudio hath wronged Hero? *(Benedick, Act 4, Scene 1)*

Enough, I am engaged… *(Benedick, Act 4, Scene 1)*

You are a villain. I jest not. *(Benedick, Act 5, Scene 1)*

I must discontinue your company. *(Benedick, Act 5, Scene 1)*

Tips for assessment

In your assessment, think about connecting the wording of the question with one of the play's themes. For example, a question about loyalty might bring you to the theme of friendship or a question about women might allow you to show your understanding of the depiction of the battle of the sexes.

Honour, pride and jealousy

The characters' senses of honour, pride and jealousy motivate much of their action. It is important to Don Pedro and Claudio that Hero is a suitable match for the count and, in his campaign against Hero, Don John says to Claudio, **'But it would better fit your honour to change your mind.'** *(Act 3, Scene 2)* When Claudio rejects Hero, Don Pedro refuses to defend her, saying **'I stand dishonour'd.'** For both characters, this is a reversal from the first scene when they returned from war, Claudio wreathed in the honour of battle and Don Pedro credited with a spectacular victory.

Leonato and his family's honour have been disgraced by Claudio's accusations. He associates the shame he feels with having previously been proud of Hero. But he is only one of many characters who exhibit pride. Some critics feel that pride or self-love is the biggest obstacle to Benedick and Beatrice's love. Each fights for the upper hand and the last word, unwilling to admit weakness, until tricked by their friends. Their pride is also assaulted during the 'gulling' scenes when their friends poke fun at their weaknesses, exposing Benedick's inability to **'modestly examine himself to see how much he is unworthy so good a lady'** *(Act 2, Scene 3)* and Hero's exclamation that 'nature never fram'd a woman's heart / Of prouder stuff than that of Beatrice' *(Act 3, Scene 1)*. Both Benedick and Beatrice, reflect on how they must change in order to be worthy of love.

Jealousy and envy are themes in other Shakespeare plays, notably *Othello* and *A Winter's Tale*. Although Don John's motivations, beyond his desire to be a villain, are not always clear, it is reasonable to assume that envy of his brother's position is one. However Claudio is the character most associated with jealousy, and Don John quickly manipulates this weakness by first suggesting that Don Pedro is wooing Hero for himself and then through the more elaborate plot suggesting Hero's infidelity.

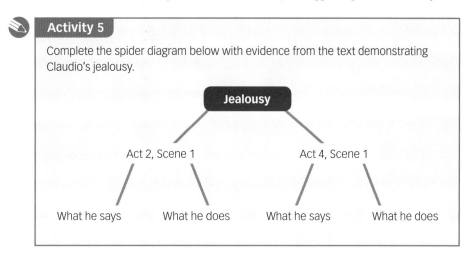

Activity 5

Complete the spider diagram below with evidence from the text demonstrating Claudio's jealousy.

Jealousy

Act 2, Scene 1

Act 4, Scene 1

What he says   What he does   What he says   What he does

Appearance, reality and deception

From the first scene, characters question what is the truth. For example, Beatrice challenges the messenger's account of Benedick's valour as a soldier and instead suggests a version of him as a fickle, faithless, greedy man. In Act 2, Scene 1, it is significant that the characters are in disguise, allowing them the opportunity to flirt or insult each other with the pretence that they don't know to whom they are speaking: 'But that my Lady Beatrice should know me, and not know me!'

Act 3, Scene 2 explores appearances, first by the playful mocking of Benedick's changed appearance, but then the more serious insinuation by Don John that Hero is not all that she appears: 'The word is too good to paint out her wickedness.' In Act 4, Scene 1, Claudio highlights the difference between Hero's innocent appearance and her apparent sinfulness: 'Out on thy seeming!' However disguise is reintroduced in the play's resolution when the female characters enter 'masked' and Claudio agrees to marry Leonato's brother's daughter, sight unseen.

Deception is used both positively and negatively in the play, both promoting and destroying love. There are also elements of self-deception such as when Benedick declares he will never marry or Dogberry asserts his status and wealth.

The women disguise their identities when Claudio has to agree to marry one of them, in the 1993 film

Key quotations

You may think I love you not. Let that appear hereafter, and aim better at me by that I now will manifest.
(Don John, Act 3, Scene 2)

Would you not swear –
All you that see her – that she were a maid,
By these exterior shows? But she is none.
(Claudio, Act 4, Scene 1)

Why seek'st thou then to cover with excuse
That which appears in proper nakedness.
(Leonato, Act 4, Scene 1)

Activity 6

Can you believe your eyes – or your ears? Write a bullet point for every time a character is deceived in the play.

Writing about themes

Upgrade

In your assessment, you may be asked to explore a particular theme or you may be given an extract in which one or more theme is presented. When writing about themes, remember to provide evidence of how language is used and the different ways the theme could be interpreted.

To prepare, you might try revising the following theme-based questions:

- What is the importance of disguise in Act 2, Scene 1?
- How is language used to explore the difference between appearance and reality in the play?
- How does Shakespeare portray different aspects of love in the play?
- How is Claudio's jealousy exploited by Don John?
- How is friendship portrayed in the play?
- To what extent does Beatrice defy traditional gender roles?
- To what extent do you agree with the following statement: 'This is a play that pits men against women.'?
- Compare and contrast the relationships between Hero and Claudio, and Benedick and Beatrice.

The Elizabethan theatre

Theatre-going was a popular activity in Elizabethan times with people from all social classes. The poor would pay a penny (roughly the cost of a loaf of bread) to stand in the 'yard' or 'pit' as one of the 'groundlings' while aristocrats would sit in the most expensive tiered and covered seats. The first performances of *Much Ado About Nothing* are thought to have been in either 1598 or 1599, probably at the Curtain Theatre in Shoreditch where Shakespeare's company, The Lord Chamberlain's Men, were performing from 1597–1599. Like the Globe Theatre, which Shakespeare's company used from the summer of 1599 onwards, the Curtain Theatre was a **polygonal** theatre, with the central area open to the sky. It housed the first performances of *Romeo and Juliet* and *Henry V* (in which it was immortalized as a 'wooden O'). *Much Ado About Nothing* remained in the company's repertoire for years and was performed at court as part of the Christmas Revels in 1612.

In the 1590s, Richard Burbage was the leading actor of the company, so may have played the role of Benedick. The leading comic actor was Will Kempe for whom the role of Dogberry was created. Kempe is also thought to have played Bottom in *A Midsummer Night's Dream*. When Kempe left Shakespeare's company in 1599, the role of Dogberry would probably have gone to Robert Armin, who played many of the later 'clown' characters with the company, in what was thought to be a more subtle and sophisticated way. All the female roles would have been performed by boy actors, as women were not permitted to perform on stage until 1660.

Actors bring the action onto the thrust stage, under the open structure of Shakespeare's Globe, London

polygonal a closed shape having many sides

Going to the theatre was very different from the experience nowadays. Performances at these outdoor theatres took place in the afternoon to take advantage of the daylight and the theatres could be noisy, crowded places with audiences interacting with the performers and each other. Shakespeare, as an actor and playwright, was aware of the demands of such an audience and ensured that there were scenes, such as Dogberry's, to please the groundlings as well as romance, danger and wit to keep the whole audience attentive. The emphasis was largely on the words (audiences would sometimes speak of going to 'hear' a play rather than to 'see' it) and the rich language of *Much Ado About Nothing* would have been appreciated. Although sets and props tended to be very simple, the costumes were often elaborate. Elizabethan audiences would enjoy seeing the ornate, fashionable clothes of the characters and would be able to understand the social messages intended by displays of certain colours and fabrics.

Activity 1

Costumes and disguises are important in *Much Ado About Nothing*. Go through the play and note any time when you think a character would need to change costumes or where an item of clothing or accessory is specified in the script (such as masks). Discuss the choices a modern costume designer might make to increase the effect of these changes for a contemporary audience.

Dramatic devices

Writing plays is very different from writing novels or poetry, and playwrights use a number of specific devices to make their intentions clear and keep the audience engaged. As you read the play, consider how characterization, comedy, suspense and resolution are achieved.

Soliloquy

A soliloquy is when a character speaks their thoughts aloud to the audience. These moments usually occur when a character is alone on stage – the word 'soliloquy' derives from the Latin, meaning to speak alone. An actor may choose to address these words very directly to the audience, or he or she may speak them as if lost in his or her own thoughts.

Activity 2

Read the following excerpt from Michael Dobson's article about Donald Sinden's performance of Benedick opposite Judi Dench in 1976, in which he describes his interpretation of Benedick's soliloquy in Act 2, Scene 3.

> Audiences remember how he would sometimes perform the whole of his soliloquy at the end of Act 2 – in which Benedick, tricked into believing Beatrice loves him, gradually abandons his former opposition to marriage – as though remonstrating with increasing vehemence with a single chosen spectator in the stalls. He would make a tremendous, emphatically nodding climax of the line 'The world must be peopled', as though this were a clinching riposte with which to convince his obdurate opponent, and would then stomp triumphantly off – only to return a moment later, visibly calming himself, to offer the same spectator amends with a placatory, face-saving 'When I said I would die a bachelor, I did not think I would live till I were married'. Dench recalls finding Sinden so funny and so perpetually unexpected that she would sometimes be laughing too much to make her ensuing entrance.

1. With a partner, try to recreate how Donald Sinden did this speech, with one of you playing Benedick and the other a member of the audience.

2. Now try acting the speech as if Benedick is totally unaware of the audience and is puzzling out his change of heart in private.

3. Discuss which interpretation you prefer and why.

4. Locate any other soliloquies in the play and write a paragraph explaining what you learn about the character speaking in each.

Dialogue

Dialogue is the conversation or words spoken between two or more characters. In *Much Ado About Nothing*, sometimes this dialogue is interrupted by asides, when the characters break off from their conversation to briefly share their thoughts with the audience or another character on stage, such as in the 'gulling' scenes. The best dialogue suits the character's personality, background and motivations, as well as furthering the action of the play.

Activity 3

1. Look at the two sections of dialogue below and see if you can correctly identify each speaker.

2. Then note the vocabulary used, the length of sentences, any indication of characterization and what the characters hope to accomplish through their words.

Dialogue 1

Character 1: Yes, I thank God, I am as honest as any man living that is an old man and no honester than I.

Character 2: Comparisons are odorous. 'Palabras', neighbour ___ .

Character 3: Neighbours, you are tedious.

Character 2: It pleases your worship to say so, but we are the poor duke's officers. But truly, for mine own part, if I were as tedious as a king I could find in my heart to bestow it all of your worship.

Dialogue 2

Character 1: [Aside] I should think this is a gull, but that the white-bearded fellow speaks it. Knavery cannot, sure, hide himself in such reverence.

Character 2: [Aside] He hath ta'en th'infection. Hold it up.

Character 3: Hath she made her affection known to Benedick?

Character 4: No, and swears she never will. That's her torment.

Stage directions

The first editions of Shakespeare's plays were compiled by actors and included a few very brief stage directions indicating entrances, exits and key moments such as fights, dances or music. Scholars cannot agree whether any of these stage directions were written by Shakespeare, were copied from a **prompt book** of an early performance or originated from another source. Other editions of the plays, including the one you are studying, have expanded these initial stage directions in order to make the action of the play easier to follow.

prompt book the complete script of a play, including additional technical information for staging the production. The 'prompter' in Shakespeare's time would fulfil the function of a modern-day stage manager

However, Shakespeare includes many indications of the actions of the play in his dialogue. For example, in Act 2, Scene 1, Leonato announces the entrance of others, **'The revellers are entering, brother'**, and clears the stage for them by saying **'Make good room.'** We also know from other dialogue in that scene that Hero and Don Pedro will 'walk' together and that it is likely that Benedick and Beatrice are doing a dance the involves following 'the leaders' and has much 'turning'.

Activity 4

Closely read Act 5, Scene 4, noting all the stage directions in your edition of the play. Then identify any lines of Shakespeare's dialogue that you think suggest certain actions or movements by the actors. For example, when Claudio says **'Give me your hand...'**, do you think he should reach out to Hero?

Physical comedy

There are many opportunities for physical comedy in scenes such as those involving Dogberry and the Watch, the masked dance of Act 2, Scene 1 or the two overhearing scenes. Directors of the play must decide how far they wish to go for the more farcical elements of the comedy or if they prefer gentler or darker humour.

The gulling scenes provide an excellent opportunity for visual humour, as shown when Beatrice hides in the 2013 film

Activity 5

1. Many productions experiment with how to extract as much humour as possible from the overhearing scenes. Read the descriptions of the following four productions' interpretations of Act 3, Scene 1 and decide which you like best.

   - In the 1973 New York Shakespeare Festival production, Beatrice hides in a conservatory to overhear her friends. They 'accidentally' soak her when they turn the sprinklers on.

   - In the 2005 Shakespeare Retold television version, Beatrice is smoking a cigarette in a toilet cubicle of a nightclub at Hero's hen night while her friends, pretending not to know she is there, stand at the ladies' room mirror and discuss her.

   - In the 2006 Royal Shakespeare Company (RSC) production set in 1950s Cuba, Beatrice's 'gulling' scene takes place in a public square where she accidentally sets off the horn on a Vespa scooter she is hiding behind and then has to turn it off.

   - In the 2015 touring Globe Theatre production of the play, Hero and Ursula are doing the laundry and douse the eavesdropping Beatrice with a bucketful of water.

2. Imagine you have been asked to direct the scene in a totally different way – how would you do it?

Staging

Shakespeare's plays were performed on a 'thrust' stage, surrounded by an audience on three sides. Theatres like the Globe held approximately 1500 people, but for popular shows it is thought that as many as 3000 people crowded in, meaning that actors had to be skilled at projecting their voices and gestures. Shakespeare wrote his plays to flow fluently from one scene to the next.

Compared to modern theatres, there was relatively little scenery or technical equipment beyond a small curtained 'discovery space', pillars and a trapdoor. For some scenes, minor set furniture or props like benches, stools, cushions or torches might be brought on. Effects like those created by music were very important and there was a musicians' gallery on the balcony at the back of the stage.

Activity 6

Go through the play and note all the times music is mentioned. Discuss how music could add to the atmosphere of the play. If you were directing the play, how would you integrate music into your concept?

The play in performance

One key to the popularity of *Much Ado About Nothing* is the casting of the roles of Benedick and Beatrice. The 18th-century actor David Garrick chose it as his first role when he returned to the stage after his marriage, adding a wry humour to the lines when he claimed to be reluctant to be married. Real-life couples who have played the roles include Maggie Smith and Robert Stephens (directed in 1965 by Franco Zeffirelli at the National Theatre) and Kenneth Branagh and Emma Thompson (the 1993 film). Directors must also make decisions on the play's setting, the time period of the play and which themes they wish to emphasize.

Stage productions

Victorian production

The most popular acting partnership in the Victorian age was that of Henry Irving and Ellen Terry who mounted a very successful production of the play in 1882, which emphasized realism and spectacle. The Act 4, Scene 1 church scene employed marble pillars, wrought-iron gates, organ music, flowers, towering candles, stained glass, incense, a painted canopy, statues and elaborate costumes to create a sense of ceremony and wonder, as well as heightening the public nature of Hero's disgrace. Ellen Terry was considered an outstanding Beatrice, with one critic noting: 'Others have had gaiety and humour, grace and vivacity, tenderness, dignity and deep feeling, but not as Ellen Terry had them.'

20th-century productions

The RSC's production of 1976 starred Donald Sinden, an accomplished comic actor in his fifties, and Judi Dench, a much respected classical actor in her forties, as two warm, witty, mature lovers. It was set in a mid-19th-century garrison in India, in the days of the British Raj.

Ellen Terry and Henry Irving thrilled Victorian London with their interpretations of Beatrice and Benedick

In 1993, Mark Rylance and Janet McTeer made a touching and unconventional pairing, described by Paul Taylor in *The Independent* as:

… a sort of Little and Large Show, for Rylance's gauche, hack-haired, bandy-legged bantam of a Benedick is a good head shorter than Janet McTeer's splendidly off-hand, Junoesque Beatrice… Instead of giving the usual showy fencing match, both actors play in a deliciously low-key manner. Even the broader farcical inventions have a lovely lightness of touch, as when, rather than be caught by his friends in romantic mode, this Benedick crams his copy of the song 'Sigh No More' into his mouth and passes off the resulting bulge as toothache. Also the moment when Benedick idiotically insists on reading love into Beatrice's every action, even though here she happens to be hacking and scoffing a banana at the time.

Catherine Tate and David Tennant in the 2011 production at Wyndham's Theatre, London

21st-century productions

In 2011, David Tennant and Catherine Tate, known particularly for their roles on television, played Benedick and Beatrice in a keenly anticipated production directed by Josie Rourke. The setting was updated to the 1980s in Gibraltar after the Falklands war. The production was praised for its inventiveness, such as the addition of a hen party for Hero where her supposed infidelity took place, and the crisp, tart chemistry between the two leads.

The RSC's 2012 bhangra-infused production was set in modern Delhi and featured Meera Syal and Paul Bhattacharjee as the reluctant lovers. The director Iqbal Khan expressed the desire to explore the themes of the play, such as chastity and arranged marriages, through the Indian setting.

The 2013 Old Vic Theatre production cast two unusually mature actors as Benedick (James Earl Jones, 82) and Beatrice (Vanessa Redgrave, 76). Set in an English village in 1944, with a US army base nearby, it used the jazz and jive-inspired music of the era and portrayed the Watch as a troupe of boy and girl scouts.

Activity 7

Choose two contrasting productions from those described above and research reviews, interviews and images from them. Create a chart comparing the productions using the headings: Actors, Location, Time period, Staging, Themes, Reviews.

Vanessa Redgrave and James Earl Jones in the 2013 production at the Old Vic Theatre

Film and television versions of the play

The demands of film-making are different from those of a stage production, so even those films based on stage productions are usually altered to make them more accessible to a film audience. When planning a film of *Much Ado About Nothing*, the director must decide how to handle the soliloquies (Should they be addressed to camera, done as voice-overs or as if the character believes he or she is alone?), whether or not to open out the scenes to multiple locations and how much of Shakespeare's language to retain.

The Joseph Papp Shakespeare in the Park stage production performed in New York City was one of the most loved 20th-century versions and was subsequently filmed, attracting a large television audience in 1973. The soldiers are in the US Calvary and their return is greeted by confetti and a marching brass band. The genteel, affluent late 19th/early 20th-century American society to which they returned is depicted in pretty pastels, with porches, swings and a carousel. Dogberry and the Watch are inspired by the early silent movie comedians, the Keystone Cops, and enter riding a Ford Model T car. The outsider, Don John, expresses his fury by shooting at ducks in a small pond and pounding angrily on a piano.

In 1993, Kenneth Branagh, who had earlier played a young Benedick on stage directed by Judi Dench, directed his wife Emma Thompson as Beatrice in the film, reprising Benedick opposite her. The sun-drenched Tuscany setting is emphasized, with the soldiers arriving on horseback while the occupants of Messina paint and picnic. Beatrice recites the lines to the song 'Sigh no more' at the film's opening, firmly allowing her to take centre stage.

In 2012, director Joss Wheedon located his film at a drink-fuelled weekend party in a luxurious Californian house. Set in the present day, the film retains the Shakespearean language, albeit with an American accent. The black and white film emphasizes some of the darker aspects of the comedy, with characters hiding in shadows and around corners. Conrad is a glamorous woman and the drinking and smoking conspirators are caught by two well-meaning but incompetent detectives wielding guns and torches.

Writing about performance

Upgrade

When writing about a play, it is important to consider the guidance provided by the playwright to shape the performance and the different ways the play can be interpreted by directors, designers and actors. However, some students become confused and simply describe a film or stage version that they have seen. You will always be expected to examine what Shakespeare has written and the dramatic devices he has used to make it effective, so ensure that you know how the production you have seen varies from what Shakespeare wrote. While revising the play, remember to do the following:

- Use the correct terminology when writing about the play, including soliloquies, asides and stage directions.

- Write about the 'audience' rather than the 'reader' and consider how a modern audience might respond to aspects differently from one in Shakespeare's time.

- Reflect on why Shakespeare structured the play in a particular way.

- Consider what is shown on stage and what is left to the audience's imagination.

- Write about how the characters' dialogue reflects aspects of their personalities and backgrounds.

- Analyse how comic and dramatic effects are achieved.

- Consider how different actors might characterize a role or how different directors emphasize particular aspects of the play.

- Explore how the director's choices might reflect the concerns of the audience, such as men returning from war, arranged marriages or the inequality of the sexes.

Skills for the assessment

Reading and studying a play like *Much Ado About Nothing* should be a pleasurable experience, but for most of you, it is leading up to something which people do not always enjoy – an assessment. Whatever the form of the assessment, it is the place where you must demonstrate your understanding of the play under the constraints of an assigned task and limited timing. However, it is important to remember that assessments are designed to allow you to exhibit your skills, not to trick you and, with proper preparation, they can be a positive experience.

Preparing for your assessment

Before your assessment, complete the following tasks to get ready:

- Make sure that you have studied at least one actual exam paper beforehand.
- Get used to quickly locating your question (often there are a number of different texts in the same paper as other schools will have studied different plays and texts).
- Know how many marks your Shakespeare question is worth and plan your timing accordingly. (Sometimes there is clear guidance in the actual exam paper with specific timings.)
- If it is an exam where you will be answering more than one question, have a plan about the order in which you might answer the questions (e.g. you might start with the one worth the most marks or the one which you are likely to find easiest).

Understanding the question

Carefully read the question and underline key words, even if you think you have answered a similar question before. Every year, students lose marks because they write about the wrong scene or character, or misunderstand the focus of the question.

Below are some typical essay-style questions, with key words and phrases underlined, each followed by an explanation of what the question requires.

Characters

> How does Shakespeare present the character of Don Pedro in the play?

This is a good example of when it is important to underline the name of the character as many students find it easy to confuse the names Don John and Don Pedro, which would have catastrophic results for this examination. The words 'how' and 'Shakespeare presents' invite you to explore the techniques Shakespeare uses, such as his imagery and dramatic devices. Sometimes these questions might use the word 'develop' rather than 'presents' which makes clear that you should choose several scenes and perhaps discuss them in chronological order.

> Explore the attitudes and feelings of Beatrice in the play.

'Explore' is a word commonly used in exams and encourages you to use your imagination and insight in your answer. When a question asks about 'attitudes' and 'feelings', you might consider how those words differ. For example, you might think about Beatrice's 'attitude' towards marriage in general and her 'feelings' towards Benedick (and how these change) in particular.

Themes

The themes are the big ideas presented in the play and to write well about them you should be able to cite more than one time that the theme is presented.

> Explore how the theme of deception is presented in the play.

You should consider exactly what 'deception' means in this play. For example, there are playful incidents of deception such as those in the 'gulling' scenes or more ominous ones such as the lies told by Don John. Remember to think about the language used in deception and any stage devices that aid its presentation.

Relationships

> Explore what we learn about the relationship between Don Pedro and Claudio in Act 1, Scene 1 and at least one other scene in the play.

This question requires you to explore two characters in relation to each other. Your first task might be to consider their words and actions to each other in the named extract and then compare and contrast that with their behaviour in another. For example, after the close confiding of Act 1, Scene 1, you could contrast this with Claudio's jealousy in Act 2, Scene 1 or their heartless argument with Antonio and Leonato in Act 5, Scene 1. You might also want to compare and contrast Don Pedro and Claudio as characters, exploring their status and use of language.

Language

> How does Shakespeare use language to present Claudio's
> repentance in Act 5, Scene 3? Compare and contrast it with
> the use of language in at least one other scene in the play.

A question that highlights language expects you to identify if the excerpt is in prose
or verse and what literary techniques, such as metaphors, similes and puns, are
being used. As always, you should point to the effect created rather than simply
identifying these devices. The language in Act 5, Scene 3 is different from that
in much of the play because there is so much rhyming verse. You might wish to
consider why Shakespeare has used formal rhyming verse in both poetry and song in
order to express Claudio's feelings. Then compare and contrast this with a scene that
uses language in a different way, such as the scene in which Benedick is tricked.

> How does Shakespeare use comedy to explore love in the play?

This question gives the opportunity to discuss how wordplay, puns, irony and
hyperbole are used to expose the love between Benedick and Beatrice. In addition
to looking at language, you could also consider how the other dramatic devices,
such as comic misunderstandings, add to the comic portrayal of love. Make sure that
you demonstrate that you understand what comedy is and the main components of
Shakespearean comedy. Similarly, the question might ask you to focus on dramatic
tension, suspense or conflict.

Planning your answer

When faced with time pressure, it is tempting to begin writing as soon as you've
opened your exam paper. However, every year, examiners report that the best
responses are those in which there is evidence of planning. The purpose of planning
is to ensure that you:

- focus on all aspects of the question
- organize your points logically
- cover a range of relevant points necessary to meet the assessment criteria
- include quotations and literary terminology
- avoid missing out key points.

The challenge for you is to take those moments to prepare your response while leaving yourself enough time to complete your answer. There is not one set way to plan an answer successfully, so you may wish to try some of the methods below to answer the following question and see what works best for you.

How is the theme of deception explored in the play?

Spider diagram

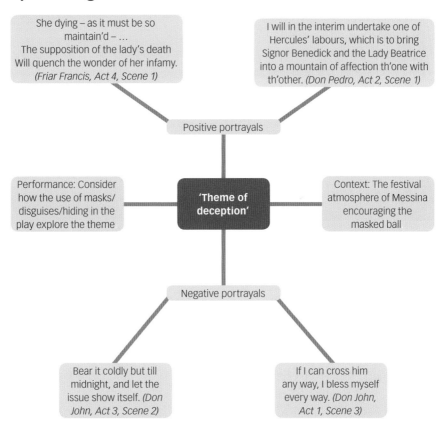

She dying – as it must be so maintain'd – …
The supposition of the lady's death Will quench the wonder of her infamy. *(Friar Francis, Act 4, Scene 1)*

I will in the interim undertake one of Hercules' labours, which is to bring Signor Benedick and the Lady Beatrice into a mountain of affection th'one with th'other. *(Don Pedro, Act 2, Scene 1)*

Positive portrayals

Performance: Consider how the use of masks/ disguises/hiding in the play explore the theme

'Theme of deception'

Context: The festival atmosphere of Messina encouraging the masked ball

Negative portrayals

Bear it coldly but till midnight, and let the issue show itself. *(Don John, Act 3, Scene 2)*

If I can cross him any way, I bless myself every way. *(Don John, Act 1, Scene 3)*

Tips for assessment

Upgrade

If you use a spider diagram for your planning, remember to group your ideas, e.g. by themes, characters, positive or negative portrayals, and so forth. You can then number the points in the order you wish to write about them.

Lists

Some students find it helpful to remind themselves of the types of points they need to cover in order to plan their response.

Theme: Compare the use of deception to create love (Benedick and Beatrice) or destroy love (Claudio and Hero.) Destroyed love regained through deceit (Friar Francis' plan).

Language: Nature imagery, oxymorons and antithesis in Act 4, Scene 1: 'rotten orange', 'impious purity'. Natural imagery used in 'gulling' scenes: 'Bait the hook well' (fishing and hunting). Puns disguise the meaning of words.

Structure and form: Misunderstandings are part of comedy. Comic deceptions accompanied by more sinister ones. Use of parallel plots.

Context: Theatricality of disguises, dramatic irony of audience being aware of the deceit. Danger of characters assuming different roles.

Tips for assessment

Upgrade

The best responses have a clear sense of argument. Make sure you begin with a strong opening sentence that shows how you are approaching the question. To avoid repetition, once you have made a point, tick or put a line through it on your plan.

Paragraphs

To help with the organization of your answer, you may want to begin thinking about shaping it into paragraphs, e.g.

Paragraph 1: How deception can be both positive and negative in the play. The comic misunderstandings bring about the love between Benedick and Beatrice but can also be destructive. (Structure/form)

Paragraph 2: Positive and comic depictions of deceit in Act 2, Scene 1: characters in disguise, Beatrice insults Benedick. The two overhearing scenes: use of hunting and fishing imagery. (Language)

Paragraph 3: Use of disguise and deceit in performance, performance choices in Act 2, Scene 1; Act 2, Scene 3; Act 3, Scene 1. (Context/interpretation)

Paragraph 4: Negative depictions of deceit: Don John (Plot/language)

Paragraph 5: Resolution through deceit: Act 5, Scene 4: Friar Francis' plan leading to 'Meantime let wonder seem familiar/and to the chapel let us presently.'

Activity 1

Choose one of the sample questions from the beginning of this chapter and use the three different methods above for creating a plan. Which method did you find most efficient and time-effective?

Writing your answer

Once you have completed your plan, which should be in note form and only take a few minutes, you need to begin your actual response. To make sure that you remain focused on the question, it is a good idea to include some of the wording of the original question in your introductory paragraph. Throughout your essay, keep returning to aspects of the set question to avoid wandering off-topic.

Your answer will be a series of paragraphs (not bullet points, which are for planning only). Each paragraph should start with a **topic sentence** that introduces the main point of the paragraph. You will then develop and support those ideas with evidence from the text. In most cases, your central paragraphs should have several quotations from the text followed by an explanation. You should end with a final paragraph tying together your ideas.

Tips for assessment

When looking over your own work, check for the following two common errors:

- Several paragraphs with no quotations from the text: this suggests that you are not providing evidence or analysing language. This is often the sign of a student who is just retelling the plot or describing a character.

- Paragraphs that end with quotations: this is often an indication of a student who is supplying evidence but forgetting to analyse the language or ways in which the lines could be interpreted.

Activity 2

Choose one of the questions at the beginning of this chapter and write a series of topic sentences you could use to start each paragraph in your answer.

topic sentence the first sentence in a paragraph, which introduces the main ideas that follow

Using quotations

Using quotations is necessary to show that you are able to select appropriate evidence from the text and analyse the language used. Extract-based questions are helpful as you will be able to choose the quotations you need from that passage. It is a good idea to annotate the extract, underlining quotations you wish to analyse and writing any helpful notes beside them (like 'metaphor' or 'contrast with later in the play'). Most exams, however, will also require you to reflect on the play as a whole, so memorizing some key quotations from the text will be useful for that.

Once you have chosen the quotations you wish to use, you should explain or analyse them. This process if often called PEE, which stands for Point, Evidence, Explanation. An example of this might be:

[Point] In Act 1, Scene 3, Don John is shown to be the villain of the piece with little evidence of his motivation for wanting to cause mischief.

[Evidence] Don John uses the metaphor of a 'canker in a hedge' to explain his hostility to Don Pedro and declares himself a 'plain-dealing villain'.

[Explanation] Rather than detailing the wrongs Don Pedro or Claudio have done to Don John, Shakespeare suggests that it is simply in Don John's nature to cause trouble. This is reinforced by his declaration that it 'fits my blood to be disdained' and he is unable to pretend to be convivial. It may be that he finds his illegitimate status limiting because he compares himself to a bird in a cage (in which he refuses to 'sing'). The figurative language in this scene creates the image of someone festering in their unhappiness with the world.

Activity 3

Read the following student's answer to a question about the presentation of Hero's character. Rewrite the answer to improve it by providing evidence and explanations.

Hero is a rather passive character who does not speak up much for herself. This is in contrast to her more outspoken cousin Beatrice. Hero is also compliant when her father arranges her marriage. The audience sees a little more of her personality in the scenes with the other female characters. Her inability to defend herself in Act 4, Scene 1 causes others to assume her guilt.

Tips for assessment

When including quotations, remember to embed them into your essay in a grammatically correct way. Do not suddenly break off from your paragraph and put in an isolated quotation. The best quotations are short and carefully chosen.

Spelling, punctuation and grammar

Your spelling, punctuation and grammar (SPaG) will be assessed in your exam and you will make a much better impression if your work is correctly written. In extreme cases, writing errors can be so severe that they can obscure the meaning, which costs many marks. When you are practising timed writings, carefully check your work for errors. Common mistakes include:

- misspelling the title of the work or the names of characters
- misusing common punctuation such as apostrophes or commas
- forgetting to punctuate quotations correctly
- writing in an overly informal way, with abbreviations such as 'u' or 'IMO'
- lack of noun/verb agreement, such as writing 'they was' or 'what Shakespeare done'
- lack of capital letters at the beginning of sentences or for proper nouns like names of characters or places
- leaving out words
- writing overly long, unshaped paragraphs.

Tips for assessment

Allow five minutes at the end of your exam to check over your work for writing errors. If you have left out punctuation or a word, insert them then.

In order to improve your writing style, try the following:

- Avoid over-use of the word 'I'. Although the examiner wants to see your engagement with the text, too much 'I feel' can lead to a lack of academic analysis.
- Vary the beginnings of your sentences.
- Vary the length of your sentences.
- Use linking or comparing phrases such as 'in contrast' or 'however' to indicate when you are showing opposing ideas.
- Use phrases like 'most significantly' or 'remarkably' to show when you want to rank or draw particular attention to an idea.

Activity 4

With a partner, take it in turns to proofread each other's writing and identify any of the common errors mentioned above. Then set yourselves targets on how to improve your work. For example, you might decide to memorize the spelling of all the characters' names in one week or use three different linking phrases in your next essay.

Sample questions

1

Read the extract from Act 2, Scene 1 below and then answer the following questions:

- How does Shakespeare portray the character of Beatrice in this extract?
- How is the role of women portrayed and developed throughout the play?

The extract from Act 2, Scene 1 starts 'He were an excellent man...' and continues to '... I had rather lie in the woollen.'

2

How does Shakespeare present relationships between family members in *Much Ado About Nothing*? Remember to provide evidence from the play and to consider its social, cultural and historical context.

3

Using the extract below as a starting point, explore the presentation of love in the play:

The extract from Act 2, Scene 1 starts 'Count, take of me my daughter...' and continues to '... and cry 'Heigh-ho for a husband.''

4

Read the extract below from Act 3, Scene 3. Then answer both parts of the following question:

- How does Shakespeare create comic effects in this scene?
- Discuss the use of comedy in the rest of the play.

The extract from Act 3, Scene 3 starts 'Are you good men and true?' and continues to '... thank God you are rid of a knave'.

5

Read the extract below from Act 1, Scene 3. Answer question (i) and then choose one of the following two questions (ii) or (iii):

i) How is the character of Don John portrayed in this scene?

Either

ii) Show how Shakespeare develops Don John's character throughout the rest of the play. Remember to provide evidence and refer to the context of the play.

OR

iii) Explore how status is shown in the play. Remember to provide evidence and refer to the context of the play.

The extract from Act 1, Scene 3 starts 'I wonder that thou...' and continues to 'Who comes here?'

6

Read Friar Francis's speech below from Act 4, Scene 1. Then answer the following questions:

- How is language used in this speech to highlight the Friar's plan?
- How is verse used in the play to emphasize different feelings and attitudes?

The extract from Act 4, Scene 1 starts 'Marry, this, well carried...' and continues to 'Out of all eyes, tongues, minds, and injuries.'

7

How is conflict portrayed in the extract below from Act 5, Scene 1 and in the play as a whole? Consider:

- the language used in this extract
- the different types of conflict presented elsewhere in the play.

The extract from Act 5, Scene 1 starts 'Marry, / Thou dost wrong me...' and continues to '... thou shalt kill a man.'

8

Referring closely to the extract from Act 5, Scene 4 below, explore:

- how marriage is portrayed in this extract
- the attitudes towards marriage presented in the rest of the play.

Remember to consider the context of the play.

The extract from Act 5, Scene 4 starts 'I'll tell thee what, Prince...' and continues to 'There is no staff more reverend than one tipped with horn.'

Sample answers

Sample answer 1

> Referring first to the extract from Act 1, Scene 1 below and then the rest of the play, explain how the character of Claudio is portrayed.
>
> *The extract from the end of Act 1, Scene 1 starts from 'O my lord' and continues to Don Pedro's line 'In practice let us put it presently.'*

Claudio is portrayed as being a young character in the play, first introduced as having done 'in the figure of a lamb the feats of a lion' to describe his successes as a soldier despite his youth. In this extract, we see that he is confiding in Don Pedro and seeking his advice on whether or not he should woo Hero. Although most of Act 1, Scene 1 is in prose, it is significant that Claudio's confession of love is in iambic pentameter as this seems to stress the romance and heightened feelings of this section.

Not a particularly strong start. It needs more insight into character.

Identifies this is verse, but needs more analysis.

Claudio separates his feelings from when he 'look'd' with a 'soldier's eye' and his 'soft and delicate desires' upon returning from war, though he does stress that even before going to war he 'lik'd her', so that the Prince doesn't think he is rushing too quickly into a marriage. To a modern audience it might seem odd that Claudio is willing to have the Prince act as a go-between ('I will break with her and with her father'), but in Elizabethan times the idea of marriage being arranged was more common and Don Pedro's high status would have added to Claudio's allure as a husband. Don Pedro uses some figurative language, which emphasizes his role in promoting Claudio's match when he says he will 'take her hearing prisoner with the force', suggesting that Hero will have little chance to object to marrying Claudio.

Makes effective and appropriate use of context.

Analyses some language, but also needs to return to the question.

Elsewhere in the play, Claudio seems to become awkward and tongue-tied with Hero, such as when Beatrice has to prompt him to speak, "tis your cue', which may suggest that Claudio was uncertain in his ability to express himself. His moodiness is also indicated by Beatrice's pun about him being 'civil as an orange', comparing him to a bitter Seville orange because of his short, negative answers to Don Pedro.

Makes valid points, but this paragraph is underdeveloped.

Shakespeare also foreshadows his tendency towards jealousy by his readiness to believe that Don Pedro has wooed 'for himself.' Once again using verse, Claudio laments this apparent betrayal and declares that 'beauty is a witch', suggesting the spell he feels Hero has cast over him and possibly other men. Benedick, like Beatrice, notices that Claudio is behaving peevishly, hitting out at all the wrong people – 'now you strike like the blind man'.

Ends with a quotation, which can suggest a lack of analysis.

However, the audience sees a different side to Claudio in Act 2, Scene 3 when he joins with Leonato and Don Pedro in tricking Benedick into thinking Beatrice has declared her love for him. Though Don Pedro takes much of the lead in setting up the deception, Claudio adds in a number of comic details and takes delight in remarking in asides at how successfully they have caught Benedick: 'Bait the hook well. This fish will bite.'

Needs more analysis of the quotation and connection to the question.

Uses well-chosen quotations and considers that Claudio can be interpreted in different ways.

In Act 4, Scene 1, there is a dangerous turn to Claudio's action when he humiliates Hero at the altar. Although some critics may feel that this is simply a sign of his immaturity and lack of experience, others find it difficult to forgive him. His language is particularly cruel: 'rotten orange,' 'savage sensuality' and the oxymoron 'impious purity'. Damaged by this experience of love, Claudio vows to 'lock up all the gates of love' for fear of experiencing this 'harm' again. He also behaves badly towards Leonato and Antonio in Act 5, Scene 1 when he seems to taunt them for being old and shows no sympathy for the trauma that Leonato, in particular, has experienced.

Perhaps aware of how negatively Claudio might be perceived by the audience, in Act 5, Scene 3, he undertakes a penance and this, in turn, leads to his happy ending when he marries Hero. As the play is a comedy, multiple weddings are called for, and Claudio and Hero, along with Benedick and Beatrice, are united in the end.

This candidate has a good understanding of the character of Claudio, selects appropriate quotations and considers some aspects of context and interpretation, but the overall response needs better organization. A stronger argument in the opening statement and then clearly organized paragraphs backing up those points would earn this a higher grade.

Sample answer 2

> Closely read the extract below from Act 1, Scene 1 and then answer the following questions:
>
> - How is the 'battle of the sexes' portrayed in this extract?
> - How does Shakespeare explore gender roles elsewhere in the play?
>
> *The extract from Act 1, Scene 1 starts 'I wonder that you will still be talking' and continues to 'You always end with a jade's trick. I know you of old.'*

The 'battle of the sexes' and the inevitable conflict between the sexes is a key theme of the play and the 'merry war' between Beatrice and Benedick is shown in their first dialogue together on stage. Shakespeare presents Beatrice and Benedick as two strong, intelligent characters who, as it is said later in the play, are 'too wise to woo peaceably'. Beatrice, in particular, is an unconventionally outspoken woman at a time when women were expected to be more subservient, so, as is clear from this extract, she is happy to take a leading role in this battle.

Opens confidently, explicitly answering the question and showing knowledge of the whole play.

Begins to consider context and gender roles.

In this prose extract, Benedick, with Don Pedro and Claudio, has returned triumphant from battle, so might reasonably expect to be met with adoration from the women left behind, which makes Beatrice's first line to him particularly insulting. After he makes a joke, Beatrice points out that 'nobody marks you', making Benedick appear foolish and insignificant. Benedick quickly returns the insult through the use of personification ('Lady Disdain', as if Beatrice is the walking embodiment of this unattractive quality of pride). He then tops it with the question 'Are you yet living?', possibly suggesting either that he thought she was so old she might have died or that whether she lived or not was of no importance to him.

Analyses her first line thoroughly, including the context.

Uses literary terminology and considers two interpretations of a line.

From this point, the 'battle' between the two characters escalates. Both use further personification of 'disdain' and 'courtesy' to score points off each other. Both characters also exhibit their antipathy towards romance. Benedick claims hyperbolically that although all women ('only you excepted') love him, he loves 'none', while Beatrice, beginning a sequence of nature imagery, claims that she would 'rather hear my dog bark at a crow than a man swear he loves me'. It might be argued that Beatrice and Benedick are protesting too much – claiming

Considers interpretation of their relationship and demonstrates understanding of the play.

that they can't stand each other, when, as the play progresses, it becomes clear that they are very ready to fall in love with each other. Although they are arguing, Shakespeare makes clear in this scene that they are a match for each other in their wit and liveliness, even if there is a threat of a 'scratching'. The dialogue ends with Beatrice's line, 'I know you of old', suggesting that their past relationship has been frustrating for her.

The characterization of Beatrice is vital in this 'battle of the sexes' because of her forthright and outspoken nature. In Elizabethan times, this role would have been played by a boy actor, but in subsequent ages, it has been an extremely popular role for actresses as it allows the opportunity to play a strong woman. She can shine using wordplay and wit, but also demonstrates that she is a loyal friend and eventually a heartfelt lover. That she is very much Benedick's equal is confirmed by the structure of the play when her 'gulling scene' follows Benedick's and their reactions mirror each other. She frequently tops him in dialogue.

A very different 'battle of the sexes' occurs in Act 4, Scene 1. First, it is clear that Hero, as a young woman, is treated very differently from the male characters. When it is thought that she is not a 'maid', she is compared to damaged goods, a 'rotten orange' and dismissed as a 'common stale' to be returned to her father. Beatrice wishes that she could fight for Hero's honour but that 'is a man's office' and she has to ask Benedick to fight on her behalf. Shakespeare uses this scene to convey the complexity of their gender roles and emotions when moments after declaring her love for Benedick she asks him to 'Kill Claudio.' This mixture of love and violence is surprising and audiences may find themselves laughing but also unsettled by her vehemence, as Benedick first seems to be when he replies, 'Not for the wide world'. Beatrice's frustration at her restricted role is made explicit when she says, 'I cannot be a man with wishing therefore I will die a woman with grieving', summing up the impossibility for a strong woman so hampered by her society's restrictions.

Makes accurate reference to performance context.

Attempts to analyse structure, but could use a little more development here.

Considers the complexity of gender roles presented in Act 4, Scene 1 with some sophistication.

This is an impressive response which demonstrates a thorough understanding of two scenes as well as relevant aspects of the context and use of language. To develop further, the candidate could consider the gender roles of the male characters and the lesser female roles such as Ursula and Margaret.

Sample answer 3

> Starting with the extract below from Act 4, Scene 2, explore Dogberry's importance in this scene and then consider the dramatic functions of Dogberry and the Watch in the rest of the play.
>
> *The extract from Act 4, Scene 2 starts 'What else, fellow?' and continues to 'O that I had been writ down an ass!'*

Dogberry is in the play to make the audience laugh and that can be seen in this extract. Conrad calls him an 'ass' and Dogberry is very insulted. However, he shouldn't be as the audience can see that this is a fair description. Dogberry tries to act like he knows what he is doing, but the Sexton has to explain to him over and over again that he is doing it wrong! Even if I don't find Dogberry funny, I can see that he is meant to be.

> Opens quite informally, especially with the exclamation mark and 'I'.

One way that Shakespeare makes Dogberry funny is when he uses malapropisms, which is when you substitute the wrong word for the one that you mean. In this extract, he says 'opinioned' when he means 'pinioned' or 'bound', and later he says 'piety' when he must mean something like 'guilt'. It seems that Dogberry wants to use big words that he doesn't understand when he could just use shorter words that make sense.

> Uses literary terminology correctly and provides examples.

One short word that he does understand is 'ass' and this is repeated six times in this scene, twice by Conrad and four times by Dogberry himself. This would be funny to the audience because it is a word they wouldn't expect him to say and then it is said repeatedly. Dogberry feels particularly worried because he would hate it to be 'written down' but then he makes it all the more memorable by stating it over and over again, like when he says 'yet forget not that I am an ass'. This repetition is one way of increasing the comedy.

> Analyses the use of repetition in detail.

Dogberry has a very high opinion of himself, which is also comic. He claims that he is good looking ('as pretty a piece of flesh') and 'a rich fellow' when it is unlikely that this is true, or at least not when compared to some of the other characters in the play. However, he likes to imagine that he is wise and powerful, and that is obvious in the way he treats the rest of the Watch.

> Needs more development and examples.

The dramatic function of Dogberry is to lighten the atmosphere after serious scenes. The scenes with Dogberry and the Watch

> Makes an accurate structure point, but could explain more.

often follow the most serious and dramatic scenes, such as after the scene when Don John says that Hero is unfaithful or after Claudio rejects her as a bride. They also provide a contrast to the upper-class characters and would have given the groundlings in the Globe Theatre characters that they could recognize and enjoy.

Makes brief but accurate context point.

The Watch are also responsible for catching Borachio and solving the mystery of the caller at Hero's window. So, in a way, you could say that they are the heroes of the play, but since they have small roles that isn't really their dramatic function. They are much more important as comedians and, in performances of the play, the actors can extend the physical comedy to make the roles even funnier.

Could consider interpretation more and give specific examples. Needs more analysis of the Watch.

In the end, Dogberry is happy because he is given both money and thanks by Leonato. This would mean a lot to him because he is someone who often gets things wrong (e.g. he gets his numbers mixed when he says 'thirdly' after 'sixth and lastly'). He is happy that for once he got things right. So the dramatic function for Dogberry and the Watch is to help bring about the happy ending for the play, to make sure the audience know it's a comedy and to give the groundlings something in particular to watch – even if all his jokes aren't particularly funny to us today.

Ends somewhat disjointedly, which could be improved by planning.

This candidate understands quite a bit about Dogberry, but expresses his ideas in too informal and unanalytical a way to achieve a really high mark. With more use of literary terminology (such as 'comic relief') and more formal analysis, starting with the idea of 'the importance of Dogberry' this would be much improved.

Glossary

antagonist a character who is hostile to another character and tries to bring about his or her downfall

allusion a mention or reference to something, such as a familiar story or classic text

antipathy intense dislike

antithesis either starting a sentence with a proposition to which the opposite is then presented or when two opposites are put together for contrasting effect , e.g. 'Come, lady, die to live' (Act 4, Scene 1)

aside when a character speaks directly to the audience, unheard by the other characters on stage

blank verse unrhymed lines of poetry with a regular metre

comedy a genre of play which emphasizes the comic and amusing aspects of the characters' lives and ends happily

comic business physical movements and gestures, sometimes involving props or set pieces, which heighten the humour of a scene

comic relief amusing scenes which provide a temporary release of tension

connotation association with a word beyond its literal meaning

cuckold a husband whose wife was unfaithful to him; a term of insult to a man, suggesting he was weak and impotent

deus ex machina a surprising and unlikely plot device which brings about a resolution to what seemed to be an impossible situation

dialogue the conversations of the characters

dissemble give a false appearance

dramatic irony when the audience knows something one or more characters on stage do not, e.g. the audience knows that Benedick's friends know he is there and that they are purposely trying to convince him that Beatrice is in love with him

falling action the events after the plot's climax which eventually lead to the resolution

foreshadow when an author hints at something which happens later

feminist critic an academic writer who analyses works, looking particularly at the portrayal of female characters and issues of inequality in gender roles

feminist icon someone who is a positive role model for women, e.g. by show of strength, intelligence or independence beyond what is expected in her society

First Folio the name given to the edition of 36 of Shakespeare's plays published in 1623, which was prepared by two actors, John Heminges and Henry Condell

gulling tricking or deceiving

Hellespont a narrow strait in Turkey, important in Greek mythology and now called the Dardanelles

Hymen the Greek god of marriage

hyperbole use of exaggeration

iambic pentameter a line of verse with ten syllables, forming five 'feet' where the stress falls on the second syllable of each foot, e.g. 'Up-<u>on</u> the <u>in</u>-stant <u>that</u> she <u>was</u> a-<u>ccus'd</u>'

imagery the use of visual or other vivid language to convey ideas or emotions

impediment an obstacle or barrier

innuendo a hint or hidden reference to something rude, often sexual

malapropism using an incorrect word for another, often creating a comic effect

malcontent a dissatisfied person, possibly one who feels grievances due to thwarted ambitions or unhappiness with the established social order

metaphor a figure of speech applied to something to suggest a resemblance, without using the words 'like' or 'as'

oxymoron a figure of speech that contains apparently contradictory ideas

parallel plots plots that are woven together and usually share some characters and themes

patriarchy a society in which men are dominant

personification when human qualities are attributed to something non-human such as objects or ideas

penitential expressing regret or requesting forgiveness for wrongdoing

plot the main events of the play

polygonal a closed shape having many sides

prompt book the complete script of a play, including additional technical information for staging the production. The 'prompter' in Shakespeare's time would fulfil the function of a modern-day stage manager

prose any writing in continuous form without rhythm or rhyme

pun a joke that relies on double meaning or similar sounds of words

redemption being forgiven for sin, atoning for a mistake or fault

repartee conversation characterized by witty replies

repetition repeating of a word in a sentence or speech

requited something returned in equal measure, such as love

rhetoric language designed to have a persuasive or impressive effect on its audience

rhetorical question a question asked for effect rather than expecting an answer

rhyming couplet two consecutive lines that rhyme, e.g. If it prove so, then loving goes by haps. / Some cupid kills with arrows, some with traps. (Act 3, Scene 1)

ribald crude humour, usually involving jokes about sex

simile a comparison between two things using the word 'like' or 'as'

soliloquy when a character is alone on stage, speaking his or her thoughts to the audience

sonnet a 14-line poem with a formal rhyme scheme. In Shakespearean sonnets, the first 12 lines rhyme alternately and then end with a rhyming couplet

stage direction part of the script, but not the speeches, which gives indications of the setting and physical actions. Editors of Shakespeare's plays use stage directions to establish entrances, exits and other key movements such as fights

sub-plot a secondary, less important plot of the play

sub-text the meaning beneath words, not directly stated

subservient submissive, willing to serve another or accept a secondary role

theme a subject or idea that is repeated or developed in a literary work

topic sentence the first sentence in a paragraph, which introduces the main ideas that follow

wordplay witty use of words to play upon their multiple or unclear meanings

OXFORD
UNIVERSITY PRESS

Great Clarendon Street, Oxford OX2 6DP United Kingdom

Oxford University Press is a department of the University of Oxford. It furthers the University's objective of excellence in research, scholarship, and education by publishing worldwide. Oxford is a registered trade mark of Oxford University Press in the UK and in certain other countries.

British Library Cataloguing in Publication Data

Data available

ISBN 978-0-19-836799-4

Kindle edition ISBN 978-0-19-836800-7

10 9 8 7 6 5 4 3 2 1

Printed in Great Britain by Bell and Bain Ltd., Glasgow

Acknowledgements

Cover: AlessandroZocc/Shutterstock; **p9:** Donald Cooper/Photostage; **p11:** Donald Cooper/Photostage; **p14:** © Mary Evans Picture Library/Alamy; **p16:** Donald Cooper/Photostage; **p19:** Donald Cooper/Photostage; **p21:** Donald Cooper/Photostage; **p27:** Donald Cooper/Photostage; **p28:** © GL Archive/Alamy; **p31:** © Moviestore collection Ltd/Alamy; **p36:** © Blue Lantern Studio/Corbis; **p41:** Donald Cooper/Photostage; **p44:** © World History Archive/Alamy; **p52:** Donald Cooper/Photostage; **p57:** Donald Cooper/Photostage; **p63:** Donald Cooper/Photostage; **p66:** © Moviestore collection Ltd/Alamy; **p68:** Photofusion/Universal Images Group via Getty Images; **p72:** © Pictorial Press Ltd/Alamy; **p74:** Time Life Pictures/Mansell/The LIFE Picture Collection/Getty Images; **p75:** Donald Cooper/Photostage; **p76:** Donald Cooper/Photostage

Extracts are taken from William Shakespeare: *Much Ado About Nothing, Oxford School Shakespeare* edited by Roma Gill (Oxford University Press, 2009).

Extract from 'The Darkness at the Heart of Much Ado' by Michael Dobson, *The Guardian*, 17 June 2011, copyright © Guardian News and Media Ltd, reprinted by permission of GNM.

Extract from 'Something Out of Nothing' by Paul Taylor, *The Independent*, 8 July 1993, copyright © The Independent 1993, reprinted by permission of ESI Media.